**Editor**
Kim Fields

**Managing Editor**
Mara Ellen Guckian

**Illustrator**
Mark Mason

**Cover Artist**
Brenda DiAntonis

**Editor in Chief**
Ina Massler Levin, M.A.

**Creative Director**
Karen J. Goldfluss, M.S. Ed.

**Art Coordinator**
Renée Mc Elwee

**Imaging**
Rosa C. See

*Publisher*

*Mary D. Smith, M.S. Ed.*

S0-BDL-777

Second Grade

# SUCCESS

Reinforce and review standards-based skills

Across-the-Curriculum Activities

**LANGUAGE ARTS**

**MATH**

**SOCIAL STUDIES**

**SCIENCE**

INCLUDES

BONUS Language Arts and Math activities to get a jump start on Third Grade!

**Author**

Susan Mackey Collins, M.Ed.

**Teacher Created Resources**
6421 Industry Way
Westminster, CA 92683
www.teachercreated.com

ISBN: 978-1-4206-2572-1

© 2011 Teacher Created Resources
Made in U.S.A.

Teacher Created Resources

# Table of Contents

# Introduction

Each time a student enters a new grade, he or she is excited to begin a new curriculum and master a plethora of new and challenging skills that come with that grade. All students are intrigued when they learn something new. Remember how fun it was when you learned to write cursive letters for the first time? Or what about the first time you conducted an experiment in the science lab? How exciting it was to see if your experiment would go the way you planned!

*Second Grade Success* is part of a series that reminds each one of us how wonderful and exciting it is to advance to a new grade. Although each grade contains required fundamentals all students need to master, we must not forget that learning itself, no matter the skill, is exciting. *Second Grade Success* helps instill the fundamentals each student will need to be successful academically, but it also captures a student's imagination and love of learning as he or she completes each skill and is ready to move on to the next one.

All lessons in the series meet the national standards desired by today's most innovative teachers. Activities in this book are perfect for the classroom teacher but can also be utilized by parents hoping to find a way to give extra practice of skills outside of the classroom. Teachers and parents can select pages that will provide additional practice with a concept, or they can choose pages to teach new concepts. *Second Grade Success* includes skills in the following areas:

• **Language Arts**　　• **Math**　　• **Social Studies**　　• **Science**

An answer key is provided for these page beginning on page 168.

*Second Grade Success* also has a special bonus section at the end to provide a jump start for third-grade skills. These bonus sections are provided in each book in the series. As teachers and parents work through the skills in each book, they can easily move on to the next grade level whenever they feel a student is ready. For the regular classroom teacher who has just finished with state testing, this extra section will help ensure all students are moving forward. This section has its own answer key on page 192.

Have a successful year!

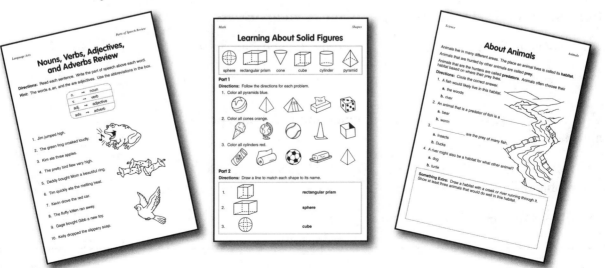

# Meeting Standards

Each lesson in *Second Grade Success* meets one or more of the following standards, which are used with permission from McREL (Copyright 2010 McREL, Mid-continent Research for Education and Learning. Telephone 303-337-0990. Website *www.mcrel.org*.)

| Language Arts Standards | Page Numbers |
| --- | --- |
| **Uses the general skills and strategies of the writing process** | |
| • Uses prewriting strategies to plan written work | 66, 69, 73 |
| • Uses strategies to draft and revise written work | 67–68, 72 |
| • Uses strategies to organize written work | 70 |
| • Uses strategies to edit and publish written work | 71, 74 |
| • Writes for different purposes | 75 |
| **Uses grammatical and mechanical conventions in written compositions** | |
| • Uses conventions of print in writing | 8–12 |
| • Uses complete sentences in written compositions | 13–14, 66 |
| • Uses nouns in written compositions | 15–19, 29–30 |
| • Uses verbs in written compositions | 20–22, 29–30 |
| • Uses adjectives in written compositions | 23–26, 29–30, 66 |
| • Uses adverbs in written compositions | 27–30 |
| • Uses conventions of spelling in written compositions | 31–33 |
| • Uses conventions of capitalization in written compositions | 38–40 |
| • Uses conventions of punctuation in written compositions | 41–52 |
| **Uses the general skills and strategies of the reading process** | |
| • Understands level-appropriate sight words and vocabulary | 34–37 |
| • Uses meaning clues | 53–56 |
| **Uses reading skills and strategies to understand and interpret a variety of literary texts** | |
| • Knows setting, main characters, main events, sequence, and problems in stories | 57–63, 65, 70 |
| • Knows the main ideas of theme of a story | 60–61 |

# Meeting Standards (cont.)

| Mathematics Standards | Page Numbers |
|---|---|
| **Uses a variety of strategies in the problem-solving process** | |
| • Uses pictures to represent problems | 76–77, 80, 93 |
| **Understands and applies basic and advanced properties of the concepts of numbers** | |
| • Counts whole numbers | 78–84, 91–92 |
| • Understands basic whole number relationships | 87–90 |
| • Understands the concept of a unit and its subdivision into equal parts | 121–122 |
| **Understands and applies basic and advanced properties of the concepts of measurement** | |
| • Understands basic concepts of time | 105–112 |
| • Knows the processes for counting money | 113–116 |
| • Knows the processes for measuring length, weight, and temperature | 117–120 |
| **Uses basic and advanced procedures while performing the processes of computation** | |
| • Estimates quantities in real-world situations | 85–86 |
| • Adds and subtracts whole numbers | 94–104 |
| **Understands and applies basic and advanced properties of the concepts of geometry** | |
| • Understands basic properties of and similarities and differences between simple geometric shapes | 123–125 |
| **Understands and applies basic and advanced properties of functions and algebra** | |
| • Extends simple patterns | 126–127 |
| **Understands and applies basic and advanced concepts of statistics and data analysis** | |
| • Collects and represents information about objects or events in simple graphs | 128–129 |

# Meeting Standards *(cont.)*

| Social Studies Standards | Page Numbers |
|---|---|
| **Geography Standards** | |
| **Understands the characteristics and uses of maps, globes, and other geographical tools and technologies** | 130–137 |
| **Understands the patterns of human settlement and their causes** | 138 |
| **History Standards** | |
| **Understands and knows how to analyze chronological relationships and patterns** | 139 |
| **Understands how democratic values came to be, and how they have been exemplified by people, events, and symbols** | 143–144, 146–147 |
| • Knows the history of American symbols | 140, 147 |
| • Knows how different groups of people in the community have taken responsibility for the common good | 145, 146 |
| **Understands the causes and nature of movements of large groups of people into and within the United States, now and long ago** | 141–142 |

# Meeting Standards *(cont.)*

| Science Standards | Page Numbers |
|---|---|
| **Understands relationships among organisms and their physical environment** | 151 |
| • Knows the basic needs of plants and animals | 149–150 |
| • Knows that plants and animals have features that help them live in different environments | 148–149, 151–152 |
| **Understands the atmospheric processes and the water cycle** | 153, 155 |
| • Knows that short-term weather conditions can change daily, and weather patterns change over the seasons | 154, 156–157 |
| **Understands the structure and properties of matter** | 158 |
| • Knows that things can be done to materials to change some of their properties, but not all materials respond the same way to what is done to them | 159–160 |
| **Understands forces and motion** | 161 |
| • Knows that position and motion of an object can be changed by pushing or pulling | 162–163 |
| **Understands the composition and structure of the universe and Earth's place in it** | 164–166 |
| • Knows basic patterns of the sun and moon | 154, 167 |

# Uppercase Letters, A–M

**Directions:** Look at each letter. Rewrite the uppercase letters on the lines provided in your best printing and cursive writing.

| | **Print** | **Cursive** | | **Print** | **Cursive** |
|---|---|---|---|---|---|
| A | | | H | | |
| B | | | I | | |
| C | | | J | | |
| D | | | K | | |
| E | | | L | | |
| F | | | M | | |
| G | | | | | |

# Uppercase Letters,  N–Z

**Directions:** Look at each letter.  Rewrite the uppercase letters on the lines provided in your best printing and cursive writing.

| | **Print** | **Cursive** | | **Print** | **Cursive** |
|---|---|---|---|---|---|
| N | | | U | | |
| O | | | V | | |
| P | | | W | | |
| Q | | | X | | |
| R | | | Y | | |
| S | | | Z | | |
| T | | | | | |

# Lowercase Letters, a–m

**Directions:** Look at each letter. Rewrite the lowercase letters on the lines provided in your best printing and cursive writing.

| | **Print** | **Cursive** | | **Print** | **Cursive** |
|---|---|---|---|---|---|
| a | | | h | | |
| b | | | i | | |
| c | | | j | | |
| d | | | k | | |
| e | | | l | | |
| f | | | m | | |
| g | | | | | |

# Lowercase Letters, n–z

**Directions:** Look at each letter. Rewrite the lowercase letters on the lines provided in your best printing and cursive writing.

| | **Print** | **Cursive** | | **Print** | **Cursive** |
|---|---|---|---|---|---|
| n | | | u | | |
| o | | | v | | |
| p | | | w | | |
| q | | | x | | |
| r | | | y | | |
| s | | | z | | |
| t | | | | | |

# Familiar Words

**Directions:** Rewrite the days of the week on the lines provided. Use your best printing and cursive writing.

**Days of the Week** _____

1. **Sunday**

2. **Monday**

3. **Tuesday**

4. **Wednesday**

5. **Thursday**

6. **Friday**

7. **Saturday**

# Writing Complete Sentences

**Directions:** Read each sentence beginning. Choose the correct sentence ending. Write the new sentence on the line.

1. I like school

    **a.** because it is fun.

    **b.** because mushrooms grow in the woods.

    **Complete sentence:** _____

    _____

2. Do you see the

    **a.** how are you?

    **b.** stars in the sky?

    **Complete sentence:** _____

    _____

3. I wish I had

    **a.** wash your hands.

    **b.** a new toy.

    **Complete sentence:** _____

    _____

4. The animals in the woods

    **a.** wanted some ketchup.

    **b.** moved quietly through the trees.

    **Complete sentence:** _____

    _____

5. Please fix our supper

    **a.** so we can hurry up and eat.

    **b.** because the chicken crossed the road.

    **Complete sentence:** _____

    _____

# Making Good Sentences

**Directions:** Read each sentence. Circle the word that best completes each sentence. Then write your choice on the line.

1. My best _____ went to the movies with me.

    **a.** friend                    **b.** scissors

2. She ate some French fries and a _____ .

    **a.** tree                      **b.** hamburger

3. How _____ will you be on your birthday?

    **a.** new                       **b.** old

4. My little sister is very _____ .

    **a.** nice                      **b.** car

5. Did you get your _____ finished?

    **a.** brush                     **b.** homework

6. I wish my _____ would put peanut butter and crackers in my lunch box.

    **a.** monkey                    **b.** mother

7. The _____ is so white and fluffy.

    **a.** rain                      **b.** snow

8. He loves seeing the zebras at the _____ .

    **a.** garage                    **b.** zoo

# Nouns, Nouns, Nouns

A **noun** is a person, place, or thing.  Show what you know about nouns by completing this page.

**Directions:**  Look at each list.  Circle the word that is a noun.

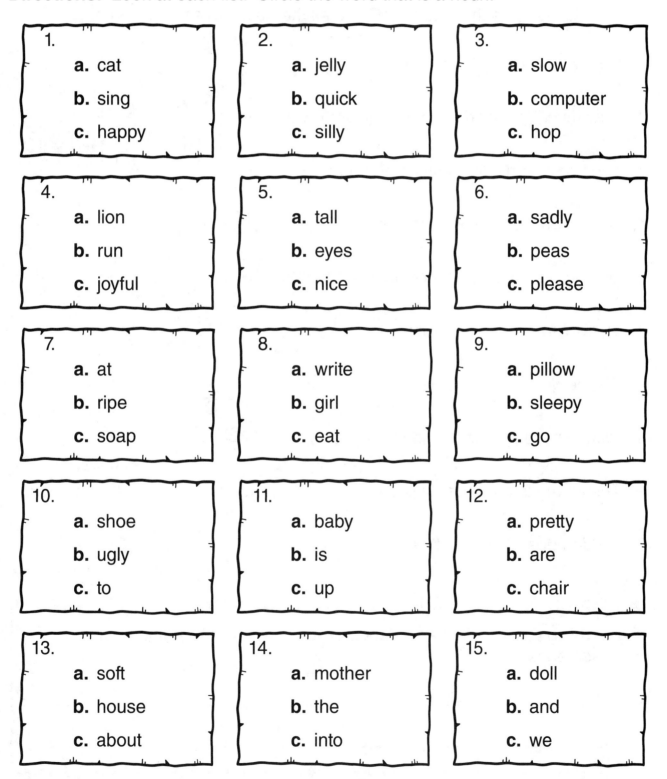

1.
  **a.** cat
  **b.** sing
  **c.** happy

2.
  **a.** jelly
  **b.** quick
  **c.** silly

3.
  **a.** slow
  **b.** computer
  **c.** hop

4.
  **a.** lion
  **b.** run
  **c.** joyful

5.
  **a.** tall
  **b.** eyes
  **c.** nice

6.
  **a.** sadly
  **b.** peas
  **c.** please

7.
  **a.** at
  **b.** ripe
  **c.** soap

8.
  **a.** write
  **b.** girl
  **c.** eat

9.
  **a.** pillow
  **b.** sleepy
  **c.** go

10.
  **a.** shoe
  **b.** ugly
  **c.** to

11.
  **a.** baby
  **b.** is
  **c.** up

12.
  **a.** pretty
  **b.** are
  **c.** chair

13.
  **a.** soft
  **b.** house
  **c.** about

14.
  **a.** mother
  **b.** the
  **c.** into

15.
  **a.** doll
  **b.** and
  **c.** we

# More Nouns

A **noun** is a person, place, or thing. All of the *people* in your family are nouns. All of the *places* you go are nouns. All of the *things* you have are nouns. Nouns are everywhere!

**Directions:** Read each sentence. Circle all the nouns in each sentence.

1. My friend is going to the circus.

2. How much money do you have in your wallet?

3. The horse and cow went into the barn.

4. Jason wanted a kitten and a fish.

5. Do you like cake, pie, or cookies the best?

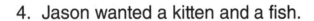

6. The doctor gave me a sticker.

7. Please give Steve your ticket.

8. Please pass the pizza and the pickles.

9. The library is a wonderful place.

10. My dog does not have fleas.

---

**Something Extra:** Write a sentence of your own. Circle all the nouns in your sentence.

_____

_____

# Know Your Nouns

**Directions:** Read each topic. Write the nouns from the Word Bank below that go with each topic.

| **Word Bank** | | | |
|---|---|---|---|
| pizza | candy | school | teacher |
| horse | lion | nurse | bread |
| store | cat | doctor | kitchen |
| bear | cheese | hospital | mother |

### Foods

1. _____

2. _____

3. _____

4. _____

### Animals

1. _____

2. _____

3. _____

4. _____

### Places

1. _____

2. _____

3. _____

4. _____

### People

1. _____

2. _____

3. _____

4. _____

**Something Extra:** Create your own category. Write four nouns under your new category.

**Category:**_____

1. _____    2. _____    3. _____    4. _____

# Singular and Plural

If something is **singular**, there is only one.  If something is **plural**, there is more than one.  Nouns can either be singular or plural.

*puppy* is a singular noun

*puppies* is a plural noun

**Directions:**  Look at each set of words.  Draw a circle around the singular noun. Write an **X** on top of the plural noun.  The first one has been done for you.

1.   **a.**  ~~dogs~~ (X)          **b.**  (dog)

2.   **a.**  cars          **b.**  car

3.   **a.**  house          **b.**  houses

4.   **a.**  pencils          **b.**  pencil

5.   **a.**  beans          **b.**  bean

6.   **a.**  plates          **b.**  plate

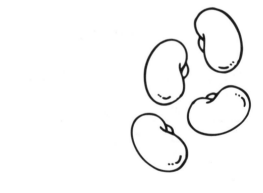

7.   **a.**  juices          **b.**  juice

8.   **a.**  apple          **b.**  apples

9.   **a.**  fans          **b.**  fan

10.   **a.**  phone          **b.**  phones

# More Singular and Plural Nouns

## Part 1

**Directions:** Read each singular noun.  Write the plural of each noun.

1. shoe  _____

2. cat  _____

3. tree  _____

4. truck  _____

5. boat  _____

6. barn  _____

## Part 2

**Directions:**  Read each plural noun.
Write the singular of each noun.

1. kids  _____

2. horses  _____

3. clocks  _____

4. plants  _____

5. baskets  _____

6. girls  _____

# Verbs "Shake" Up

A **verb** is a word that can show action. Do you ever run, hop, skip, or jump? All of these words are verbs.

**Directions:** Color the milk shake in each set that has the action verb.

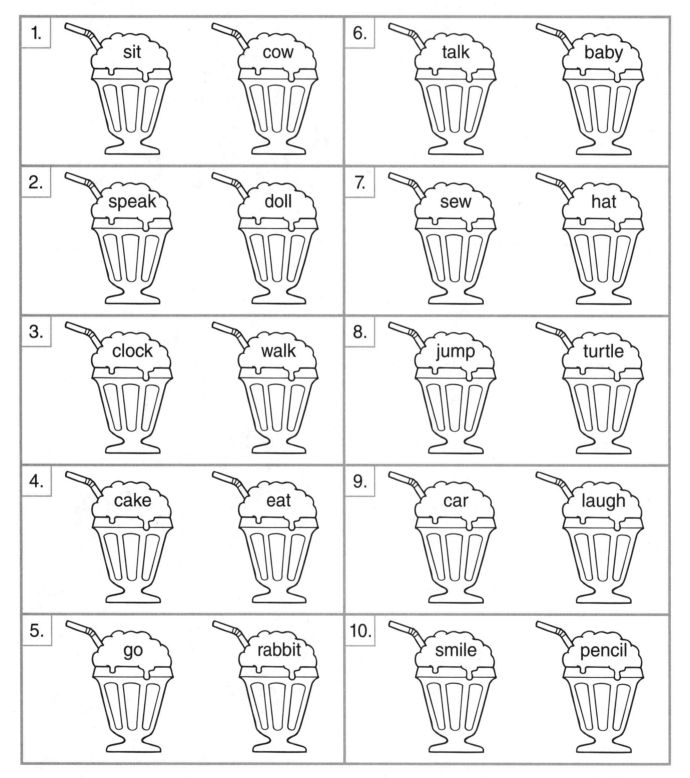

1. sit / cow
2. speak / doll
3. clock / walk
4. cake / eat
5. go / rabbit
6. talk / baby
7. sew / hat
8. jump / turtle
9. car / laugh
10. smile / pencil

# 3, 2, 1…Action!

Some verbs are action words. *Hop, skip,* and *run* are all examples of action verbs.

**Directions:** Look at each DVD case. Circle the action verb in each movie title.

1. Run with the Wind
2. Walk Across the Moon
3. Take My Hand
4. Tell Me a Secret
5. Time Moves Slowly
6. Go Dog
7. Watch Me
8. Jump High
9. Sit, Puppy!
10. Cry Little Baby

# Hidden Verbs

**Directions:** Color the egg in each set that has a verb written on it.

1.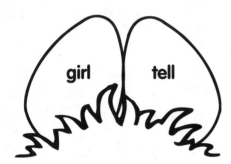

girl  tell

6.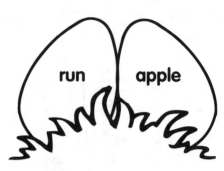

run  apple

2.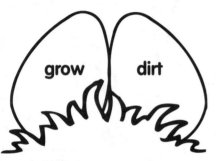

grow  dirt

7.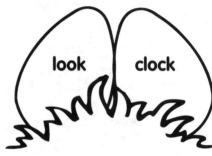

look  clock

3.

make  cookie

8.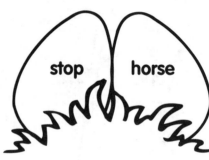

stop  horse

4.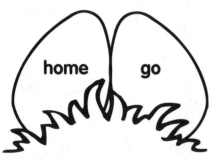

home  go

9.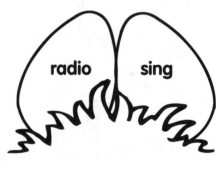

radio  sing

5.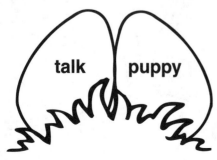

talk  puppy

10.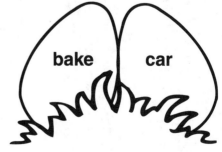

bake  car

# Adding Adjectives

An **adjective** is a word that describes.

> **Examples**
>
> *pretty* girl        *best* friend        *wonderful* surprise

**Directions:** Use the Word Bank below to help you add adjectives to the sentences below.  Use each word only once.  Each sentence has a hint to help you find the right adjective.

| **Word Bank** | | | |
|---|---|---|---|
| beautiful | happy | fluffy | nice |
| mean | helpful | short | sweet |

1. I was very h __ __ __ __ when my parents got me a puppy.

2. The __ __ __ f __ __ bunny hopped across the yard.

3. My new teacher was __ i __ __ to us when she gave us a treat.

4. The chocolate was __ w __ __ __ and delicious.

5. The flowers are so __ __ __ __ __ __ __ u __ and colorful!

6. I am so __ h __ __ __ that I can't reach the cabinet.

7. My friend was __ __ __ p __ __ __ when he taught me how to tie my shoe.

8. The __ e __ __ girl yelled at my sister.

# "Hop to It" Adjectives

**Adjectives** are words that describe or tell about other words. Adjectives describe nouns and pronouns. An adjective might tell how *crunchy* a carrot is or how *furry* a rabbit is. An adjective tells how many, which one, or what kind about a noun or pronoun.

**Directions:** Look at each pair of carrots. Color only the carrot that has an adjective written on it.

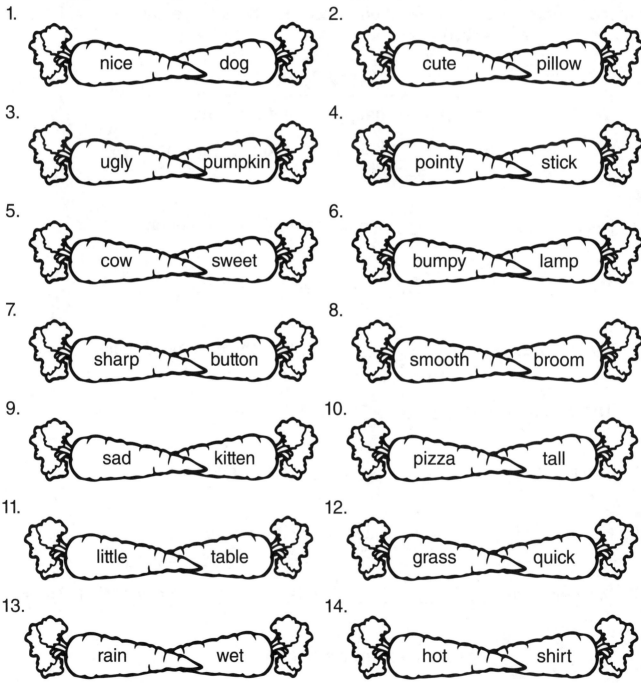

1. nice / dog

2. cute / pillow

3. ugly / pumpkin

4. pointy / stick

5. cow / sweet

6. bumpy / lamp

7. sharp / button

8. smooth / broom

9. sad / kitten

10. pizza / tall

11. little / table

12. grass / quick

13. rain / wet

14. hot / shirt

# Read and Circle Adjectives

## Part 1

**Directions:** Read each sentence and circle the adjective that best completes it.

1. I like the (new, slippery) car my brother drives.

2. My (mean, best) friend is going with me to the movies.

3. My favorite ice cream is (sweet, rotten) and yummy.

4. The (stormy, calm) weather was so bad we had to cancel the picnic.

5. Please use a (leaky, red) pen to grade your paper.

6. The (fluffy, rough) bunny made a wonderful pet.

## Part 2

**Directions:** Draw and color a picture that shows an example of each adjective.

| 1. | 2. |
|---|---|
| long | bright |
| 3. | 4. |
| pretty | tiny |

# Funny Adjectives

**Directions:** Look at the list of words. Color only the funny faces that are next to words that can be adjectives.

1. ugly   2. sweet

3. girl   4. run

5. silly   6. salty

7. nice   8. mother

9. sunny   10. tiny

11. short   12. funny

13. pizza   14. bright

15. cow   16. dark

17. shiny   18. plant

# Working with Adverbs

**Adverbs** tell *how, when, where,* and *why* about verbs, adjectives, and other adverbs. An adverb might tell that a runner ran *quickly* or that the other runner ran *slowly.* Adverbs usually end in "y" or "ly."

## Part 1

**Directions:** Circle the adverb that best completes each sentence. Write the correct word on the line.

1. He was _____ happy.

   **a.** nice        **b.** very

2. She is _____ short to reach the top shelf.

   **a.** too        **b.** quickly

3. She whispered _____ in the library.

   **a.** quietly        **b.** very

4. The elevator went up and then back _____.

   **a.** sideways        **b.** down

5. Please put your books over _____.

   **a.** where        **b.** there

## Part 2

**Directions:** Use the following adverbs in three sentences of your own: *very, slowly, here.*

1. _____

   _____

2. _____

   _____

3. _____

   _____

# Awesome Adverbs

**Adverbs** are one of the eight parts of speech.  Adverbs answer the questions *how, when, where,* and *why*.

**Directions:**  The sentences in the box tell a story.  Read the sentences and then answer the questions below.

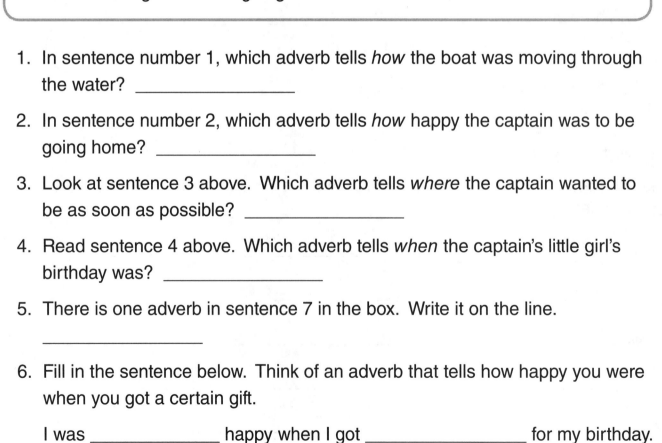

1.  The boat moved swiftly through the water.

2.  The captain was so happy to be going home.

3.  He wanted to be there as soon as possible.

4.  Today was his little girl's birthday.

5.  He had brought her a doll all the way from China!

6.  He knew the doll would make his daughter too happy for words.

7.  He was so glad he was going home.


1.  In sentence number 1, which adverb tells *how* the boat was moving through the water? _____

2.  In sentence number 2, which adverb tells *how* happy the captain was to be going home? _____

3.  Look at sentence 3 above.  Which adverb tells *where* the captain wanted to be as soon as possible? _____

4.  Read sentence 4 above.  Which adverb tells *when* the captain's little girl's birthday was? _____

5.  There is one adverb in sentence 7 in the box.  Write it on the line.

    _____

6.  Fill in the sentence below.  Think of an adverb that tells how happy you were when you got a certain gift.

    I was _____ happy when I got _____ for my birthday.
            (adverb)                        (noun)

# Nouns, Verbs, Adjectives, and Adverbs Review

**Directions:** Read each sentence. Write the part of speech above each word.

**Hint:** The words *a, an,* and *the* are adjectives. Use the abbreviations in the box.

| n. | → | noun |
| v. | → | verb |
| adj. | → | adjective |
| adv. | → | adverb |

1. Jim jumped high.

2. The green frog croaked loudly.

3. Kim ate three apples.

4. The pretty bird flew very high.

5. Daddy bought Mom a beautiful ring.

6. Tim quickly ate the melting treat.

7. Kevin drove the red car.

8. The fluffy kitten ran away.

9. Gage bought Gibb a new toy.

10. Kelly dropped the slippery soap.

# More Parts of Speech Review

**Directions:** Look at the words in the Word Bank below.

Write each **noun** on a petal of the noun flower.

Write each **verb** on a petal of the verb flower.

Write each **adjective** on a petal of the adjective flower.

Write each **adverb** on a petal of the adverb flower.

| Word Bank | | | | | | | |
|---|---|---|---|---|---|---|---|
| monkey | boy | slowly | funny | pretty | very | go | jump |
| run | swim | quickly | silly | man | too | nice | cow |

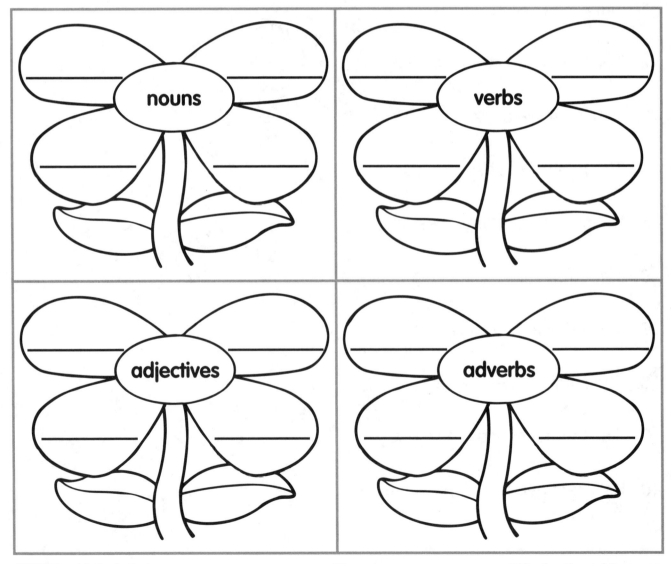

# Spelling Practice

**Directions:** Look at the basket of cherries.  Color each cherry that has a word that is spelled correctly.  Rewrite the misspelled words on the lines below.

_____        _____

_____        _____

_____        _____

_____        _____

# Look It Up

A **dictionary** gives definitions of words, but it can also help you spell words.  A dictionary is organized alphabetically.  The word **alphabetically** means it is organized from A through Z just like the alphabet.  Words that start with an "a" would be first and words that start with a "z" would be last.

**Directions:**  Below is a list of misspelled words.  Use a dictionary to look up the correct way to spell each word.  Then write the definition of each word.

| Word | Correct Spelling | Definition |
|------|------------------|------------|

1. aireplane

2. juglar

3. aple

4. oranje

5. onyon

6. puppie

# Long Vowels and Short Vowels

## Part 1

**Directions:** Read each set of words. Draw a blue circle around the word that has a long vowel sound. Draw a red circle around the word that has a short vowel sound.

| | |
|---|---|
| **1.**    **a.** brake    **b.** chop | **2.**    **a.** bake    **b.** set |
| **3.**    **a.** side    **b.** chip | **4.**    **a.** tip    **b.** tide |
| **5.**    **a.** kid    **b.** time | **6.**    **a.** bite    **b.** sip |
| **7.**    **a.** kite    **b.** big | **8.**    **a.** dip    **b.** cake |

## Part 2

**Directions:** Write two words that have a long vowel sound. Write two words that have a short vowel sound.

| 1. **Long Vowel Sound** | 2. **Short Vowel Sound** |
|---|---|
| **a.** _____ | **a.** _____ |
| **b.** _____ | **b.** _____ |

# Synonyms

A **synonym** is a word that has nearly the same meaning as another word.

> **Examples**
>
> small *and* little     quick *and* fast

**Directions:** Read each sentence. Use the Word Bank below to find a synonym for each underlined word. Write it on the line.

| Word Bank | | |
|---|---|---|
| large | faster | wonderful |
| near | kind | whole |

1. Please don't sit so <u>close</u> to me.

   **Synonym:** _____

2. Today is a <u>great</u> day!

   **Synonym:** _____

3. I ate the <u>entire</u> piece of cake.

   **Synonym:** _____

4. These clothes are too <u>big</u> for me.

   **Synonym:** _____

5. The rabbit was <u>quicker</u> than the fox.

   **Synonym:** _____

6. She is such a <u>nice</u> teacher.

   **Synonym:** _____

# Antonyms

**Antonyms** are words that have opposite meanings.

> **Examples**
>
> big *and* small      nice *and* mean

**Directions:** Circle the antonyms in each sentence. Write them on the lines below.

1. I am very little, but my sister is very big.

   _____     _____

2. My mother is nice, and she is never mean.

   _____     _____

3. The fast car went around the slow car.

   _____     _____

4. I like sweet and sour chicken.

   _____     _____

5. Some colors are dull, and some colors are shiny.

   _____     _____

6. The first test was hard, but the second test was easy.

   _____     _____

7. The elevator went up, and then it went down.

   _____     _____

8. He never eats mustard, but he always eats ketchup.

   _____     _____

9. She felt nervous at first, but then she felt calm.

   _____     _____

10. He was glad he got a puppy, but he was sad his birthday was over.

    _____     _____

# Synonyms and Antonyms

**Directions:** Circle the correct answer.

1. Little and big are _____ .

   **a.** antonyms

   **b.** synonyms

2. Pretty and ugly are _____ .

   **a.** antonyms

   **b.** synonyms

3. Nice and kind are _____ .

   **a.** antonyms

   **b.** synonyms

4. Shiny and dull are _____ .

   **a.** antonyms

   **b.** synonyms

5. Up and down are _____ .

   **a.** antonyms

   **b.** synonyms

6. Lost and missing are _____ .

   **a.** antonyms

   **b.** synonyms

7. Happy and glad are _____ .

   **a.** antonyms

   **b.** synonyms

8. Short and tall are _____ .

   **a.** antonyms

   **b.** synonyms

# Vocabulary in Context

**Directions:** Use context clues to help choose the correct word for each blank.
Circle the answer. Then write the word on the line.

1. My mother _____ me a new dress.

   **a.** bought          **b.** colored          **c.** ran

2. Yesterday we went to the theater and saw a _____.

   **a.** swim          **b.** movie          **c.** slowly

3. The _____ was shining brightly in the blue sky.

   **a.** cloud          **b.** dog          **c.** sun

4. We ate _____ and ice cream on my birthday.

   **a.** cake          **b.** sweet          **c.** summer

5. I hope it does not _____ on the carnival.

   **a.** jump          **b.** rain          **c.** cry

6. We went swimming in the swimming _____.

   **a.** washer          **b.** cow          **c.** pool

7. Please turn the television _____.

   **a.** sky          **b.** off          **c.** supper

8. I went to the party with my _____ friend.

   **a.** best          **b.** car          **c.** green

# Colorful Capitals

Always capitalize a person's name.

> **Examples**
>
> Alice Davidson          Karen Elizabeth Jones
>
> Mr. Binkley              Doctor Brown

**Directions:** Look at the balls. Color only the balls that have names that are correctly capitalized. Correct the words that need capital letters in the other balls. Use editing marks. The first ball has been done for you.

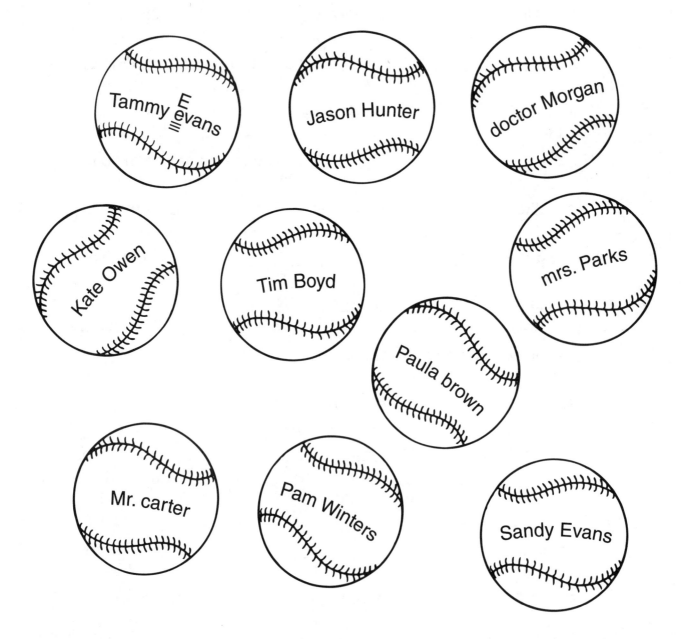

# Correct Capitalization

Always capitalize the first word of a sentence.

**Directions:** Rewrite each sentence. Capitalize the first word of each sentence.

1. i don't know what time it is.

   _____

   _____

2. she is a very nice person.

   _____

   _____

3. can we go to the playground?

   _____

   _____

4. today is a beautiful day.

   _____

   _____

5. how old are you?

   _____

   _____

# Capitalization Rules!

When you write, there are capitalization rules you need to follow.

Capitalize the first word of a sentence.

Always capitalize specific names.

**Directions:** There are two capitalization mistakes in each sentence below. Circle the capitalization mistakes and then write the words correctly on the lines.

1. she is married to dr. Mike.

    **a.** _____

    **b.** _____

2. when is lisa's party?

    **a.** _____

    **b.** _____

3. i wish sandy would let me borrow her book.

    **a.** _____

    **b.** _____

4. my dog's name is spencer.

    **a.** _____

    **b.** _____

5. can carla go to the movies with us?

    **a.** _____

    **b.** _____

# Know How to End It

A **declarative sentence** ends with a period.  A declarative sentence is a statement.

> **Examples**
>
> You are very nice.
>
> I want to go eat ice cream.

## Part 1

**Directions:**  Add the correct ending punctuation to each sentence.

1.  Today is my birthday_____

2.  Her favorite color is red_____

3.  My brother is nine years old_____

4.  I wished on a star_____

5.  She is my mother_____

## Part 2

**Directions:**  Write three declarative sentences of your own.  Add the correct ending punctuation.

1.  _____

    _____

2.  _____

    _____

3.  _____

    _____

# Use a Question Mark

An **interrogative sentence** must have a question mark. An interrogative sentence is a sentence that asks a question.

> **Examples**
>
> Do you know where my toothbrush is?
>
> What bus do you ride?

## Part 1

**Directions:** Add the correct ending punctuation to each sentence.

1. What time does the football game start_____

2. How many brothers do you have_____

3. Where did you put your bicycle_____

4. What are we having for dessert_____

5. Do you have my money_____

## Part 2

**Directions:** Write three interrogative sentences of your own. Add the correct ending punctuation.

1. _____

   _____

2. _____

   _____

3. _____

   _____

# Ending Punctuation Review

**Directions:** Read each sentence. Add the correct ending punctuation.

1. Do you want to go with me to the store____

2. January is the first month of the year____

3. My best friend's name is Sam____

4. Do you know when you are going on your trip____

5. On Friday we went to the zoo____

6. The firefighter came to talk to our class____

7. Where do you want to go camping____

8. You are my best friend_____

9. My mother's name is Jane____

10. Did you go to the dentist____

# Using a Comma

A comma is a punctuation mark that is different from ending punctuation. A **comma** is a pause in a sentence. It is not a stop at the end of the sentence.

A comma is used to separate items in a series. Use a comma if there are three or more items in a list.

> **Examples**
>
> She is funny, nice, and sweet.
>
> My mother bought me a ball, a bat, and a glove.

**Directions:** Read each sentence. Add commas where they are needed.

1. I went to the math class reading class and spelling class.

2. Please bring me my coat my umbrella and my purse.

3. My favorite days are Friday Saturday and Sunday.

4. June July and August are summer months.

5. Mercury Venus and Earth are planets that are close to the sun.

6. Red orange and yellow are all colors in the rainbow.

7. Please get some milk donuts and cereal at the store.

8. For camping you will need a sleeping bag a flashlight and some food.

9. Three people I admire are my mother my father and my grandmother.

10. After school we need to stop at the post office the grocery store and the bank.

# The Amazing Apostrophe

An **apostrophe** can be used to join two words together to make a new word. When two words join together and form a new word, it is called a **contraction**.

> **Examples**
>
> it  +  is  =  it's
>
> are +  not =  aren't

**Directions:** Look at the word sets and use an apostrophe to form a contraction.

1. he      +    is      _____

2. she     +    is      _____

3. has     +    not     _____

4. will    +    not     _____

5. he      +    had     _____

6. should  +    have    _____

7. would   +    have    _____

8. they    +    are     _____

9. I       +    am      _____

10. they   +    will    _____

# Finding the Right Contraction

**Directions:** Read each sentence. Circle the contraction that best completes each sentence. Write the correct choice on the line.

1. I _____ find my backpack.

    **a.** can't

    **b.** isn't

2. Karen _____ be able to go to the movies because she has homework.

    **a.** isn't

    **b.** won't

3. _____ my best friend.

    **a.** She'll

    **b.** You're

4. Did you know _____ going to Florida on vacation?

    **a.** they're

    **b.** she'll

5. I think _____ one of the nicest people I know.

    **a.** she's

    **b.** he'd

6. I _____ finished my homework.

    **a.** couldn't

    **b.** haven't

7. _____ so tired today!

    **a.** I'm

    **b.** we've

8. When _____ time to go, I'll let you know.

    **a.** you're

    **b.** it's

# Commas in a Series

Use commas to separate items in a series.

**Directions:** Add a beginning to each sentence. Then add commas where they are needed.

> **Examples**
>
> donuts, pancakes, and bacon
>
> My favorite breakfast foods are donuts, pancakes, and bacon.

1. _____ dogs fish and turtles.

2. _____ pizza hamburgers and hot dogs.

3. _____ red white and blue.

4. _____ October November and December.

5. _____ Florida California and Texas.

6. _____ small tiny and little.

7. _____ pants shirts and shoes.

8. _____ gum candy and mints.

9. _____ helicopters airplanes and hot air balloons.

10. _____ eyes nose and mouth.

# Separate Items in a Series

Use commas to separate items in a series. There must be more than two items to need commas.

> **Examples**
>
> I like pizza and spaghetti. ➜ No commas needed.
>
> I like pizza, spaghetti, and lasagna. ➜ Commas are needed.

**Directions:** Add commas as needed to each sentence. If a sentence does not need commas, write **C** for correct on the line provided.

_____ 1. She is nice sweet and pretty.

_____ 2. He is my best friend.

_____ 3. I have lived in Texas Utah and Virginia.

_____ 4. My favorite subjects are art math and music.

_____ 5. Are you going to invite Mark and Amanda?

_____ 6. My favorite numbers are three eight and nine.

_____ 7. The teacher asked us to bring our books our pencils and our papers.

_____ 8. James and Rusty are going to the party.

_____ 9. January February and March are very cold months.

_____ 10. I wish I could have a cat a dog and a hamster.

# Proofread for Commas

**Directions:** Read the story below. Add commas only to the sentences that have a 🐸 frog in front of them.

## The Talking Frog

🐸 Once upon a time, there was a sweet beautiful young princess named Leiana. Leiana liked to be outside. 🐸 She loved the butterflies the flowers and the sunshine. She wished she could always be in the sunshine.

One day Leiana decided to take a walk outside. She saw many things on her walk. 🐸 She saw some birds one snake and a brown rabbit. She wished she could be like the animals she met. 🐸 She wished she could stay outside all the time like the lucky birds snakes and rabbits.

Leiana walked to the big pond. She said aloud, "I wish I could always be outside and never have to go back to the castle."

You can imagine how surprised Leiana was when a frog that was sitting beside the pond began talking to her. The frog said, "You must be Princess Leiana. I am Fanny the frog. I am a magical frog. I can grant you one wish, but you must give me something in return."

"That would be wonderful!" Leiana cried. 🐸 "I could give you jewels silver or gold. Just tell me what you want."

"I want to change places with you, Princess Leiana."

Leiana looked at the frog and then looked back at the castle. 🐸 If she changed places with the frog, she could be outside in the winter spring summer and fall. She would finally have what she had always wanted.

That night only Princess Fanny, the new princess, returned to the castle. 🐸 The cook thought it odd that the princess wanted flies bugs and worms for supper, but of course, he didn't say anything.

And what about Princess Leiana? 🐸 Well, that night she croaked and croaked and croaked with joy because she finally had everything she had always wanted!

# Commas with Dates

Use a comma between the day of the month and the year. Do not put a comma between the month and the day of the month.

> **Examples**
>
> May, 12, 1876  ➜  incorrect
>
> May 12, 1876  ➜  correct

**Directions:** Place commas where they belong. Rewrite the dates.

1. April 26 1930 _____

2. June 8 1991 _____

3. September 12 2000 _____

4. March 3 1997 _____

5. December 28 1966 _____

6. July 4 1776_____

7. January 1 2009 _____

8. February 19 1967_____

9. October 27 2005 _____

10. August 3 1918 _____

11. May 15 1945 _____

12. November 10 1772 _____

# More Commas and Dates

**Directions:** Read each sentence. Add commas as needed.

> **Examples**
> On September 1, 2007, my sister got married.
> The date of my anniversary is April 7, 2000.

1. I was born on February 25 2001.

2. School started on August 4 2008.

3. The picture was taken March 7 1981.

4. The war began on April 7 1939.

5. The date on the coin was January 5 1977.

6. December 25 1977 is the date of my parents' anniversary.

7. He plans to graduate from high school on May 3 2011.

8. Her grandmother was born on February 25 1911.

9. July 4 1776 is an important date in America's history.

10. The movie was shown for the first time on March 4 1999.

11. Jane flew on a plane for the first time on June 18 2007.

12. The last time the circus came to town was July 15 2009.

# Commas with Cities and States

Use a comma between the city and the state.

> **Examples**
>
> Williamsburg, Virginia
>
> Nashville, Tennessee

**Directions:** Add commas where they are needed.

1. Austin Texas

2. Hollywood California

3. Seattle Washington

4. Memphis Tennessee

5. Louisville Kentucky

6. Ogden Utah

7. Las Vegas Nevada

8. Atlanta Georgia

9. Destin Florida

10. St. Louis Missouri

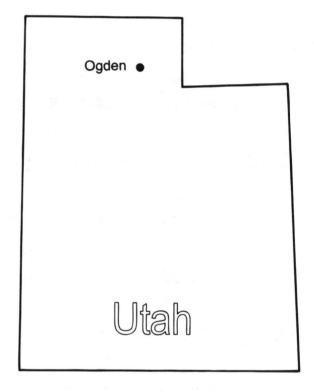

**Something Extra:** Write the name of the city and state where you live. Add commas as needed.

_____

# A Picture Is Worth…

**Directions:** List 10 facts you can learn from looking at the scene below.

> **Example**
>
> There are pigs on the farm.

1. _____
2. _____
3. _____
4. _____
5. _____
6. _____
7. _____
8. _____
9. _____
10. _____

# What's the Scene?

**Directions:** Look at each scene. Describe what is happening in each picture.

# Look for the Answers

**Directions:** Look at the magazine cover. Then answer the questions.

1. What is the name of the magazine?

   _____

2. On what page will you find information about cats and dogs getting along with each other? _____

3. What volume number is this magazine? _____

4. What can you learn if you read the article on page 48?

   _____

5. Why do you think the puppy on the cover has a bow around its neck?

   _____

   _____

# Picture the Meaning

**Directions:** Read the story below. Use the picture clues to figure out what word should be in the story. Write the word on the line.

Once upon a time there was a little  named Allison. Allison

had a pet  named Lucky. Allison and her  Lucky went

everywhere together. One day Allison was playing on the .

She would fly up and down going faster and faster. Suddenly Allison fell

off the . Lucky ran over to check on Allison. Allison had landed

on a big pile of . She was just fine. Allison stood up with a big

smile on her face. She petted her  Lucky and then said, "Well, it

looks like you and I are both lucky!"

## Answers

1. _____     2. _____

3. _____     4. _____

# Setting

A story's **setting** is where and when the story happens. Think about where you are right now. That is your own setting!

**Directions:** Look at each picture. Write the setting for each picture.

1.

Setting: _____

_____

2.

Setting: _____

_____

3.

Hillview Elementary

Setting: _____

_____

4.

Setting: _____

_____

5.

Setting: _____

_____

6.

Setting: _____

_____

# All About Setting

A setting is *where* and *when* something happens.

**Directions:** Answer each question to learn more about different settings.

1. Where might you go to buy groceries? _____

2. What time would be a good bedtime for someone your age? _____

3. Where would you go to see a new movie? _____

4. What time do you usually get up? _____

5. Where would you go to have your teeth cleaned? _____

6. Where would you go to check out a book? _____

7. Where might you go to mail a letter? _____

8. Where could you go if you wanted to go swimming? _____

9. What time does your school start? _____

10. In what month is your birthday? _____

# Describing a Story's Characters

Story characters are an important part of all stories. Characters can be human, but they do not have to be. Sometimes the main characters might be animals or even things that are created or made from the writer's imagination.

**Directions:** Read the descriptions. Draw a character to match each one.

| | |
|---|---|
| 1. Draw a small, brown, furry animal with a long tail, four legs, two pointy ears, and brown eyes. | 2. Draw a beautiful fairy princess with long red hair, two fairy wings, a magic wand, and a lovely dress. |
| 3. Draw a little boy who is wearing a baseball uniform. He is wearing the number 8 on his uniform. He has blond hair and blue eyes. | 4. Draw a character you create. Use your imagination. |

# The Main Event

The **main event** in a story is the main thing that happens.  In the story, "The Three Little Pigs," the main event is the wolf trying to eat the pigs.  In the story, "Goldilocks and the Three Bears," the main event is the bears finding Goldilocks in their home.

**Directions:**  Look at each picture.  Write what main event is going on in each one.

1.

The main event: _____

_____

2.

The main event: _____

_____

3.

The main event: _____

_____

4.

The main event: _____

_____

# Understanding the Main Idea

**Directions:** Read the story below. Then circle the correct answer for each question.

## The Camping Trip

Robert and Dale were going to have a campout in Robert's backyard. Robert's dad helped him put up the tent. Robert could not wait to go camping.

Dale was excited when he got to Robert's house. Dale knew they were going to have a lot of fun. Dale had his flashlight, his sleeping bag, and his pillow.

That night the boys settled down to sleep in the tent. Dale had turned off his flashlight. He snuggled into his sleeping bag. Robert got into his sleeping bag. Then the boys heard a noise outside the tent. They both were scared.

Dale grabbed his flashlight and turned on the light. The boys heard the noise again. They peeked outside the tent. Dale moved the light around the yard. Then they heard the noise again! The noise was closer now. What could it be? All of a sudden, Robert's dog came around the corner. Both boys laughed when they realized what the noise was. They let Robert's dog inside the tent and then went to sleep.

1. What is the main idea of the story?

    **a.** Robert and Dale are going to have a

    **b.** Robert and Dale are best friends.

2. How does Dale feel about going to Ro

    **a.** He feels nervous about going to Robert's hou

    **b.** He feels excited about going to Robert's house.

3. What does Dale bring with him for the camping trip?

    **a.** a flashlight, a sleeping bag, and a pillow

    **b.** a flashlight, some food, and a teddy bear

4. What is the noise in the night?

    **a.** a raccoon                **b.** a dog

# Sequence of Events

A **sequence** is the order in which things go.  Use what you know about sequencing to complete the activity below.

## Part 1

**Directions:**  Finish each sequence.

1. 1, 2, 3, ___, ___, ___

2. January, February, March, _____, _____,

   _____

3. A, B, C, ____, ____, ____

4. winter, spring, _____, _____

5. Sunday, Monday, Tuesday, Wednesday, _____,

   _____, _____

## Part 2

**Directions:**  Think about the mornings you get ready for school.  List five things you do to get ready on those mornings.  List them in the correct order or **sequence** that you do each one.

1. First, I_____

2. Next, I_____

3. After that, I _____

4. Then, I _____

5. Finally, I _____

# All in Order

**Directions:** Read each set of directions. Rewrite the directions in the sequence or order they should go.

1. **How to Brush Your Teeth**

    **a.** Rinse the toothpaste from your mouth.

    **b.** Put the toothpaste on the brush.

    **c.** Get out your toothbrush.

    **d.** Begin brushing your teeth.

    **Correct Sequence**

    1. _____

    2. _____

    3. _____

    4. _____

2. **How to Mail a Letter**

    **a.** Put the letter in the envelope and add the outside address.

    **b.** Write the letter.

    **c.** Place the letter in the post office box to be mailed.

    **d.** Seal the envelope and add a stamp.

    **Correct Sequence**

    1. _____

    2. _____

    3. _____

    4. _____

# Alphabetical Order

**Directions:** Write each set of words in alphabetical order.

1.

apple          _____

acre           _____

ant            _____

acorn          _____

animal         _____

2.

summer         _____

sand           _____

spin           _____

seven          _____

stop           _____

3.

table          _____

triangle       _____

tree           _____

tiger          _____

time           _____

4.

car            _____

call           _____

clam           _____

collar         _____

camp           _____

# Understanding Order

**Directions:** Look at the pictures below.

Draw a circle around the picture that happened *first* in each row.

Draw a square around the picture that happened *second* in each row.

Color the picture that happened *third* in each row.

# Start Writing

Use the activities below to help you get started writing.

## Part 1

**Directions:** In the space below, draw a picture of your favorite animal.

HW 67+68
46

## Part 2

**Directions:** List six words that descri___ ___ animal.

1. _____    2. _____

3. _____    4. _____

5. _____    6. _____

## Part 3

**Directions:** Write two complete sentences about your animal.

1. _____

   _____

2. _____

   _____

# Making Good Sense

**Directions:** Match each sentence beginning to the best sentence ending. Write the new sentences on the lines below.

| Sentence Beginnings | Sentence Endings |
| --- | --- |
| My new puppy jumped | the ice cream. |
| The little boy ate | soccer and softball. |
| The monkey swung | onto my lap. |
| My sister plays | from a vine. |

1. _____

_____

2. _____

_____

3. _____

_____

4. _____

_____

**Something Extra:** Write two of your own "sentence beginnings." Have a classmate finish the sentences.

1. _____

2. _____

# Word Wise

**Directions:** Each sentence has one word that needs to be removed. Find the word that does not belong. Draw an **X** on the word. Then write the word that does not belong on the owl by each sentence.

1. Do you want to sit by kite me?

2. I cake had a wonderful birthday party!

3. Where tree is my coat?

4. He rode his bicycle box to school.

5. I like walk apples and oranges.

6. I have two black airplane kittens.

7. The fish swam in the road ocean.

# Prewriting for a Story

Before you write a story, you should have a plan. One way to do this is to complete a story map.

**Directions:** Write a fiction story (make-believe) about a trip that someone took. Use the space below to help map out the story.

**Story Title:** _____

1. The main characters would be _____

   _____

2. The characters would take a trip to _____

   _____

3. There is a problem while they are on the trip. The problem is _____

   _____

   _____

4. The problem is solved when _____

   _____

   _____

5. At the end of the story, the characters decide to _____

   _____

   _____

# Beginning, Middle, End

Good stories have a clear beginning, middle, and end. Use the activity below to help you organize your writing.

**Directions:** Read the story. Answer the questions that follow.

## The Sunny Day

Kim and Kelly were so happy it was Saturday. Their mother had promised they would go to the playground and play all day. Kim loved the swings. Kelly loved the slide. It was going to be a lot of fun.

When Kim and Kelly woke up on Saturday, it was raining. They were so sad because they knew they could not go to the playground. The girls went to talk to their mother. Their mother was smiling at them both. "Kim and Kelly, today was supposed to be our special day. Don't be sad because it is raining. We are still going to have a special day."

Kim and Kelly's mother took them out to the garage. She had set up a play area in the garage. She had hula hoops and roller skates and even an area for bouncing balls. There were no swings or slides, but Kim and Kelly did not care. It was suddenly a sunny day after all!

1. What happens at the beginning of the story? _____

_____

_____

2. What happens at the middle of the story? _____

_____

_____

3. What happens at the end of the story? _____

_____

_____

**Something Extra:** At the end of the story, the girls decide it is a sunny day even though it is raining. Explain why the girls think that.

# Find the Mistakes

**Directions:** Below is a poster for a school carnival. The poster has seven capitalization mistakes. Circle each mistake. Write the correct capital letter above each circle.

## School Carnival

**When:** friday and saturday

december 11 and 12

4:00 pm – 8:00 pm

**Where:** San pedro Middle School
at the school's cafeteria

All money raised will go to elizabeth Smith's family to help with her hospital bills. Please come to the carnival to help this wonderful family.

---

**Something Extra:** Can you think of any other information that should have been included on the flyer? Write your answer on the line below.

_____

_____

_____

# Out of Order

When something is not working, you say it is "out of order." Writing can be out of order, too. Sometimes what is written just does not work right!

**Directions:** The writing below is out of order. Use the lines to put it back into the order it needs to be.

## How to Make a Peanut Butter and Jelly Sandwich

1. Spread the peanut butter and jelly on the bread.

2. Put the two pieces of bread together.

3. Find the ingredients you need for your sandwich.

4. Get out two pieces of bread.

## How to Make a Peanut Butter and Jelly Sandwich

1. _____

   _____

2. _____

   _____

3. _____

   _____

4. _____

   _____

# All Around

You can practice writing by writing about what you know.  Look around the room you are in.  Look at what is around you.  Now complete the activity below.

## Part 1

**Directions:** List five things you see in the room.

1. _____

2. _____

3. _____

4. _____

5. _____

## Part 2

**Directions:** Pretend you are writing a note to a family member.  In the space below, describe the room you are writing from.  Include at least four things you listed in Part I.

Dear _____,

You should see this room! _____

_____

_____

_____

_____

_____

_____

# Making Lists

**Directions:** Each chart has one thing that should not be on the list. Write the one thing that should not be on the list on the line. Be ready to explain each answer to a classmate.

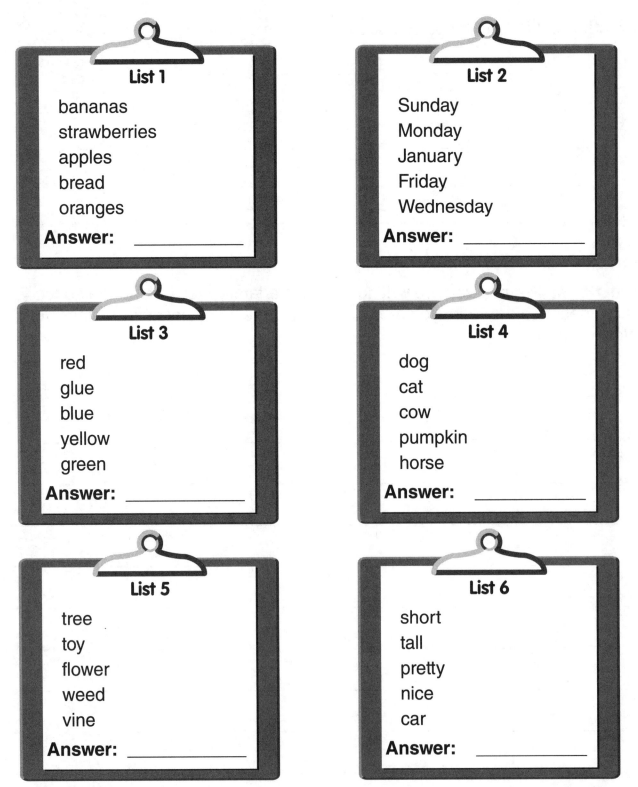

**List 1**

bananas
strawberries
apples
bread
oranges
**Answer:** _____

**List 2**

Sunday
Monday
January
Friday
Wednesday
**Answer:** _____

**List 3**

red
glue
blue
yellow
green
**Answer:** _____

**List 4**

dog
cat
cow
pumpkin
horse
**Answer:** _____

**List 5**

tree
toy
flower
weed
vine
**Answer:** _____

**List 6**

short
tall
pretty
nice
car
**Answer:** _____

# Why It Is Written

People write for many reasons. Sometimes people write to entertain other people. Sometimes people write to give information about something. Sometimes people write so other people will learn something new.

**Directions:** Read each passage below. Circle the correct answer.

---

**1.** There will be a meeting in the library at 8:00 A.M. for all Birthday Club members. Please come hungry. Birthday cake will be served.

This was written _____ .

    **a.** to entertain        **b.** to give information

    **c.** to teach something new

---

**2.** There are only eight planets in our solar system. Your parents probably learned there were nine planets. However, Pluto is no longer considered a planet. Pluto was once the last outer planet.

This was written _____ .

    **a.** to entertain        **b.** to give information

    **c.** to teach something new

---

**3.** When I was a little boy, I went fishing at a big pond. I sneaked into my daddy's tackle box, and I took a fake worm from his box to use on my hook. I didn't figure my daddy would ever find out. When I was done fishing, I would just put the worm back in his box. How surprised I was to find out there was a snapping turtle living in our fishing pond! That turtle bit my hook and bit my daddy's worm right off that hook. I don't know if that turtle had a belly ache or not from eating that plastic worm, but I know I sure did when I wondered how I was going to tell my daddy what had happened!

This was written _____ .

    **a.** to entertain

    **b.** to give information

    **c.** to teach something new

---

**Something Extra:** On the back of this page, draw a picture to show what happened in the story in #3.

---

# Look and Count

**Directions:** Count the pictures to find the total.

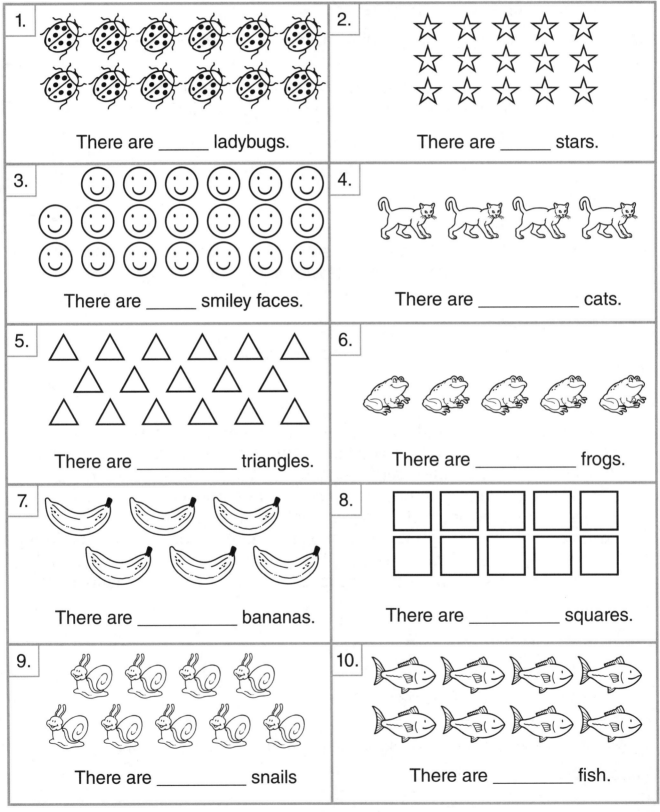

1. There are _____ ladybugs.

2. There are _____ stars.

3. There are _____ smiley faces.

4. There are _____ cats.

5. There are _____ triangles.

6. There are _____ frogs.

7. There are _____ bananas.

8. There are _____ squares.

9. There are _____ snails

10. There are _____ fish.

76

# Show the Number

**Directions:** Draw pictures to show the number that is given. Write the name of what you have drawn on the line.

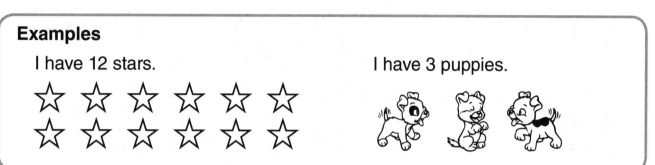

**Examples**

I have 12 stars.

I have 3 puppies.

1.

I have 8 _____.

2.

I have 2 _____.

3.

I have 7 _____.

4.

I have 10 _____.

5.

I have 9 _____.

6.

I have 5 _____.

# Counting by Ones

**Directions:** Fill in the blanks to count by ones.

1.

   1　2　___　4　5　___　___

2.

   10　11　12　___　___　___　16

3.

   7　___　9　___　11　___　13

4.

   20　21　___　23　___　25　___

5.

   15　___　___　___　19　20　___

6.

   33　___　35　___　37　___　39

7.

   18　___　20　___　22　___　___

8.

   45　46　___　48　___　___　___

9.

   ___　40　___　42　___　44　___

10.

   ___　51　52　___　___　55　___

# Count by Fives

**Directions:** Fill in the blanks to count by fives.

1.   ___   ___ ___

10  15  ___  25  ___  ___

2. 40  ___  50  55  ___  ___

3. 5  ___  15  ___  25  ___

4. 30  35  ___  ___  50  ___

5. 65  ___  75  ___  ___  ___

6. ___  30  ___  40  45  ___

7. 5  ___  15  ___  25  ___

8. 75  ___  85  ___  95  ___

9. 45  ___  55  ___  ___  70

10. 10  15  ___  ___  30  ___

# Practice Counting by Fives

## Part 1

**Directions:** Color the groups that can be counted by fives.

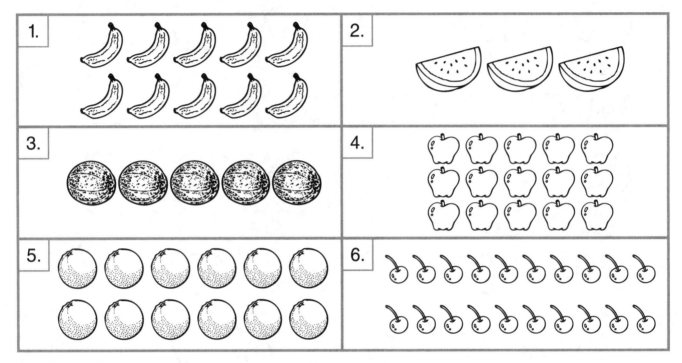

## Part 2

**Directions:** Draw and color your own groups of fives.

| 1. | Draw five jelly beans. | 2. | Draw 10 squares. |
|---|---|---|---|

| 3. | Draw 15 hearts. |
|---|---|

# Count by Tens

**Directions:** Fill in the blanks to count by tens.

1.   20, _____, 40, _____, 60

2.   10, 20, 30, _____, 50, _____, 70

3.   45, _____, 65, 75, _____, 95

4.   30, _____, _____, 60

5.   25, 35, _____, 55, _____, 75

6.   50, _____, 70, _____, 90

7.   15, 25, _____, _____, 55

8.   70, _____, _____, 100

9.   12, 22, 32, _____, 52, _____, 72

10.  40, _____, 60, _____, 80

# Practice Counting by Tens

**Directions:** Count by tens to solve each word problem.

---

**1.** Carrie has 10 worms. She wants to go fishing. Sabrina has 10 worms. She wants to go fishing, too. When the girls go fishing together, how many worms do they have to use for bait?

**Answer:** _____

---

**2.** Isaiah collects baseball cards. He has 40 cards. Carl collects baseball cards, too. He has 30 cards. How many baseball cards do Isaiah and Carl have?

**Answer:** _____

---

**3.** Anai has 20 pennies. Her grandmother gives her 10 more pennies. How many pennies does Anai have now?

**Answer:** _____

---

**4.** Tina loves to eat jelly beans. She ate 10 jelly beans for dessert at lunch. After supper she and her sister, Maria, ate 40 more jelly beans. How many jelly beans were eaten?

**Answer:** _____

---

**5.** Tommy is building a tower. He has 40 blocks. His brother, Jesse, gives him 30 more blocks. How many blocks does Tommy have for his tower?

**Answer:** _____

---

# Backward Counting

To **count by fives** backward, subtract five each time.

> **Example**
>
> 20 → 15 → 10 → 5

To **count by tens** backward, subtract 10 each time.

> **Example**
>
> 55 → 45 → 35 → 25

## Part 1

**Directions:** Count backward by **fives** to complete the pattern.

1. 75, _____, 65, _____, 55

2. 15, _____, 5

3. 30, 25, _____, 15, 10

4. 45, _____, 35, _____, 25

5. 60, 55, _____, 45, _____, 35

## Part 2

**Directions:** Count backward by **tens** to complete the pattern.

1. 75, _____, 55, _____, 35

2. 90, 80, _____, _____, 50

3. 65, _____, 45, _____, 25

4. 77, 67, _____, 47, _____, 27

5. 95, _____, 75, _____, 55

# Even and Odd Numbers

**Even** numbers can be counted in pairs or by twos.

Even numbers are **2, 4, 6, 8,** and **10**.

**Odd** numbers do not make pairs.

Odd numbers are **1, 3, 5, 7,** and **9**.

**Directions:** Look at each number. If the number is even, write an **E** on the line. If the number is odd, write an **O** on the line.

| a.     7 <br> ___ | b.     6 <br> ___ | c.     8 <br> ___ |
|---|---|---|
| d.     15 <br> ___ | e.     20 <br> ___ | f.     33 <br> ___ |
| g.     3 <br> ___ | h.     4 <br> ___ | i.     1 <br> ___ |
| j.     17 <br> ___ | k.     8 <br> ___ | l.     5 <br> ___ |

# Guessing the Number

When you **estimate** a number, you guess how many there are instead of counting every single item.

**Directions:** Estimate the number of smiley faces in each box. Circle your estimate.

**1.**
        10       30       50

**2.**
        10       30       50

**3.**
        10       30       50

**4.**
        10       30       50

**5.**
        10       30       50

**6.**
        10       30       50

# Guess the Amount

**Directions:** Estimate or guess how many items are in each group. Use the key to help you with your estimating.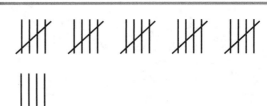

**1.**

Estimate: _____

**2.**

Estimate: _____

**3.**

Estimate: _____

**4.**

Estimate: _____

**5.**

Estimate: _____

**6.**

Estimate: _____

**7.**

Estimate: _____

**8.**

Estimate: _____

# Which Is More?

Some numbers are **greater** or more than other numbers. To show that a number is greater than another, use this symbol **>**. To show a number is **less**, use this symbol **<**.

> **Examples**
>
> 10 is greater than 8, so 10 > 8
>
> 8 is less than 10, so 8 < 10

**Directions:** Look at the number pictures. Use the > (greater than) or < (less than) sign to show the relationship between each set.

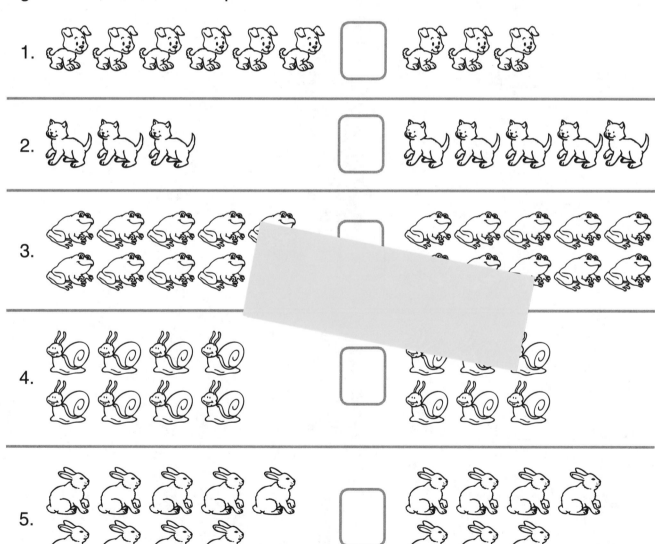

# Greater or Less Than?

Use the **>** (greater than) sign to show a number is m   than another number.

> **Example:** 17 > 5

Use the **<** (less than) sign to show a number i     other number.

> **Example:**

**Directions:** Look at each number set.       > sign to show the relationship between the numbers.

**1.** 18 _____ 23

**2.** 37 _____ 57

**3.** 7 _____ 3

**4.** 12 _____ 44

**5.** 30 _____ 13

**6.** 3 _____ 19

**7.** 10 _____ 12

**8.** 16 _____ 14

**9.** 28 _____ 40

**10.** 2 _____ 11

# Number Position

Numbers go in order.  Think about a number line.

```
  •    •    •    •    •    •    •    •    •    •
  1    2    3    4    5    6    7    8    9   10
```

You can see 1 comes *before* 2.  You can see 2 comes *after* 1.  You can see 2 comes *between* 1 and 3.

**Directions:**  Look at each row of numbers.  Follow each direction.

**1.**  7   8   9   10   11   12   13   14   15   16

    **a.** Circle the number that comes before 8.

    **b.** Draw an X on the number that comes after 14.

    **c.** Draw squares around the numbers that come between 9 and 13.

**2.**  1   2   3   4   5

    **a.** What number comes after 4?  _____

    **b.** What number comes before 2?  _____

    **c.** What numbers come between 1 and 5?  _____

**3.**  20   21   22   23   24   25

    **a.** Draw an X on the number that comes between 20 and 22.

    **b.** Draw a circle around the number that comes before 21.

    **c.** Draw a triangle around the number that comes after 21.

# Learning Before, Between, and After

**Directions:** Answer the questions for each set of numbers.

**1.**

10,   20,   30,   40,   50

**a.** Which numbers come before 30? _____

**b.** Which numbers come after 20? _____

**c.** Which number comes between 10 and 30? _____

**2.**

1,   2,   3,   4,   5

**a.** Which number comes between 3 and 5? _____

**b.** Which numbers come after 3? _____

**c.** Which number comes between 1 and 3? _____

**3.**

5,   10,   15,   20,   25

**a.** Which numbers come after 10? _____

**b.** Which number comes before 10? _____

**c.** Which numbers come between 5 and 25? _____

**4.**

20,   21,   22,   23,   24

**a.** Which number comes between 20 and 22? _____

**b.** Which numbers come after 21? _____

**c.** Which numbers come before 22? _____

# Types of Numbers

Two types of numbers are cardinal numbers and ordinal numbers.

**Cardinal numbers** tell how many of something there are.

> **Examples**
>
> There are 2 birds.     There are 5 eggs.

**Ordinal numbers** tell what order things are in or what rank something has.

> **Examples**
>
> James won 1st (first) place at the fair.
> Tina finished 3rd (third) in the race.

## Part 1

**Directions:** Write the correct **ordinal** number.

1. Candy won the race. She came in _____ place.

2. Ty had a glass of milk. He asked the waitress for another glass of milk. This would be his _____ glass of milk.

3. Kelly, Lisa, and Katherine entered the baking contest. They were the only three to enter the contest. Kelly got first place. Lisa won second place. Katherine won _____ place.

## Part 2

**Directions:** Write the correct **cardinal** number.

1. Count the number of apples in the basket. How many apples are in the basket?

   _____

2. Count the ants going to the picnic. How many ants are there?

   _____

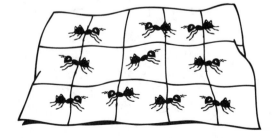

3. How many questions are on this page?

   _____

# Showing Rank

**Ordinal numbers** show rank or position.

> **Examples**
>
> She was my *first* (1st) grade teacher.
>
> She was the *second* (2nd) tallest person in the class.

**Directions:** Look at each row of fruit.

—Draw an **X** on every first picture.

—Draw a circle around the second piece of fruit in each row.

—Color the third piece of fruit in every row.

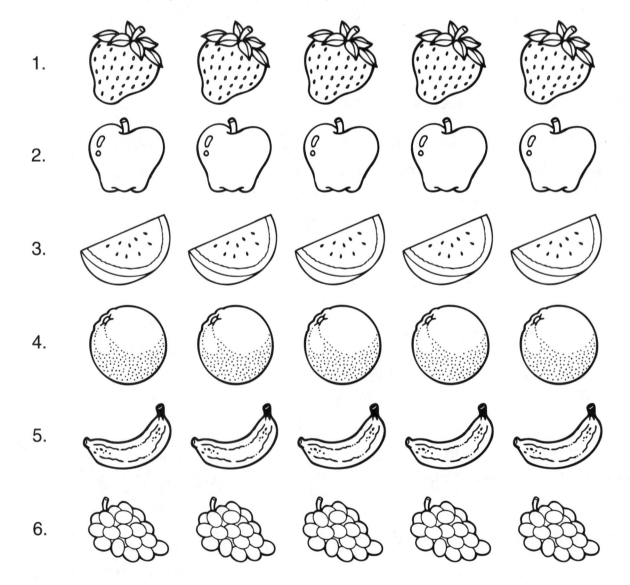

# Picture Addition

Use pictures to help understand addition.

Count the number of stars in the first group.

Count the number of stars in the second group.

What is the sum of both sets of stars?

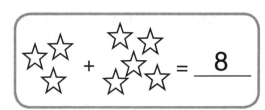

You have just added two sets of numbers! Isn't addition easy?

**Directions:** Count the pictures to find the sum. Write the sum after the equal sign.

1. = ____

2. + = ____

3. + = ____

4. + = ____

5. + = ____

6. + = ____

---

**Something Extra:** Draw your own picture addition problem on the back. Ask a classmate to find the sum.

# Blown Away with Addition!

**Directions:** Add the numbers to find the sum in each bubble.

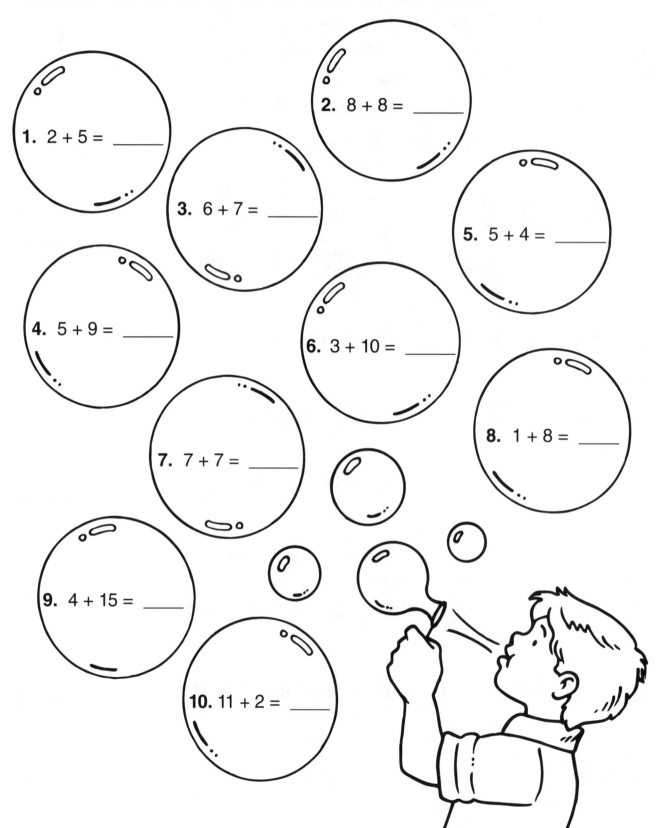

**1.** 2 + 5 = _____

**2.** 8 + 8 = _____

**3.** 6 + 7 = _____

**4.** 5 + 9 = _____

**5.** 5 + 4 = _____

**6.** 3 + 10 = _____

**7.** 7 + 7 = _____

**8.** 1 + 8 = _____

**9.** 4 + 15 = _____

**10.** 11 + 2 = _____

# Either Way, It's the Same!

**Directions:** Add the numbers to find each sum.

| | |
|---|---|
| **1.** $1 + 7 = $ _____ <br><br> $7 + 1 = $ _____ | **2.** $6 + 8 = $ _____ <br><br> $8 + 6 = $ _____ |
| **3.** $4 + 5 = $ _____ <br><br> $5 + 4 = $ _____ | **4.** $10 + 7 = $ _____ <br><br> $7 + 10 = $ _____ |
| **5.** $3 + 2 = $ _____ <br><br> $2 + 3 = $ _____ | **6.** $5 + 9 = $ _____ <br><br> $9 + 5 = $ _____ |
| **7.** $4 + 3 = $ _____ <br><br> $3 + 4 = $ _____ | **8.** $3 + 8 = $ _____ <br><br> $8 + 3 = $ _____ |

# Double-Digit Addition

**Directions:** Practice double-digit addition by finding each sum.

| | | |
|---|---|---|
| **1.**<br><br>$\begin{array}{r} 33 \\ +\ 12 \\ \hline \end{array}$ | **2.**<br><br>$\begin{array}{r} 12 \\ +\ 35 \\ \hline \end{array}$ | **3.**<br><br>$\begin{array}{r} 20 \\ +\ 55 \\ \hline \end{array}$ |
| **4.**<br><br>$\begin{array}{r} 70 \\ +\ 10 \\ \hline \end{array}$ | **5.**<br><br>$\begin{array}{r} 15 \\ +\ 23 \\ \hline \end{array}$ | **6.**<br><br>$\begin{array}{r} 63 \\ +\ 36 \\ \hline \end{array}$ |
| **7.**<br><br>$\begin{array}{r} 51 \\ +\ 18 \\ \hline \end{array}$ | **8.**<br><br>$\begin{array}{r} 48 \\ +\ 41 \\ \hline \end{array}$ | **9.**<br><br>$\begin{array}{r} 18 \\ +\ 11 \\ \hline \end{array}$ |
| **10.**<br><br>$\begin{array}{r} 78 \\ +\ 20 \\ \hline \end{array}$ | **11.**<br><br>$\begin{array}{r} 40 \\ +\ 27 \\ \hline \end{array}$ | **12.**<br><br>$\begin{array}{r} 49 \\ +\ 40 \\ \hline \end{array}$ |

# Triple-Digit Addition

## Part 1

**Directions:** Practice triple-digit addition by finding each sum.

1.
$$\begin{array}{r} 278 \\ + 211 \\ \hline \end{array}$$

2.
$$\begin{array}{r} 458 \\ + 341 \\ \hline \end{array}$$

3.
$$\begin{array}{r} 190 \\ + 100 \\ \hline \end{array}$$

4.
$$\begin{array}{r} 501 \\ + 417 \\ \hline \end{array}$$

5.
$$\begin{array}{r} 792 \\ + 202 \\ \hline \end{array}$$

6.
$$\begin{array}{r} 333 \\ + 333 \\ \hline \end{array}$$

7.
$$\begin{array}{r} 216 \\ + 102 \\ \hline \end{array}$$

8.
$$\begin{array}{r} 629 \\ + 210 \\ \hline \end{array}$$

9.
$$\begin{array}{r} 176 \\ + 123 \\ \hline \end{array}$$

10.
$$\begin{array}{r} 643 \\ + 345 \\ \hline \end{array}$$

11.
$$\begin{array}{r} 874 \\ + 121 \\ \hline \end{array}$$

12.
$$\begin{array}{r} 481 \\ + 400 \\ \hline \end{array}$$

## Part 2

**Directions:** Solve the word problem below.

The second grade class at Pleasant View Elementary has 239 students. The third-grade class at the school has 210 students. How many total students are there in the second and third grade classes?

**Show your work:**

**Answer:** _____

# Calculate the Single-Digit Subtraction

**Directions:** Solve the single-digit subtraction problems.

**1.**

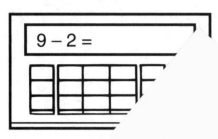

$9 - 2 =$

**2.**

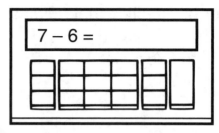

$7 - 6 =$

**3.**

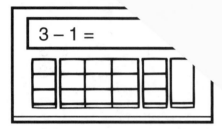

$3 - 1 =$

**4.**

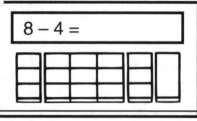

$8 - 4 =$

**5.**

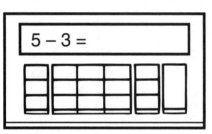

$5 - 3 =$

**6.**

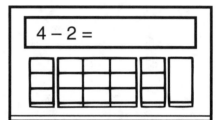

$4 - 2 =$

**7.**

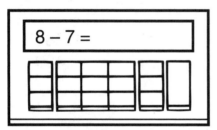

$8 - 7 =$

**8.**

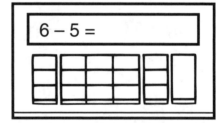

$6 - 5 =$

**9.**

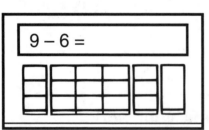

$9 - 6 =$

**10.**

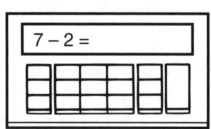

$7 - 2 =$

**11.**

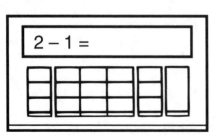

$2 - 1 =$

**12.**

$6 - 3 =$

# Double-Digit Subtraction Fun

## Part 1

**Directions:** Solve the double-digit subtraction problems.

| | | |
|---|---|---|
| 1. $\begin{array}{r} 39 \\ -\ 19 \\ \hline \end{array}$ | 2. $\begin{array}{r} 81 \\ -\ 30 \\ \hline \end{array}$ | 3. $\begin{array}{r} 75 \\ -\ 42 \\ \hline \end{array}$ |
| 4. $\begin{array}{r} 66 \\ -\ 32 \\ \hline \end{array}$ | 5. $\begin{array}{r} 28 \\ -\ 17 \\ \hline \end{array}$ | 6. $\begin{array}{r} 49 \\ -\ 22 \\ \hline \end{array}$ |
| 7. $\begin{array}{r} 99 \\ -\ 37 \\ \hline \end{array}$ | 8. $\begin{array}{r} 70 \\ -\ 60 \\ \hline \end{array}$ | 9. $\begin{array}{r} 18 \\ -\ 12 \\ \hline \end{array}$ |
| 10. $\begin{array}{r} 88 \\ -\ 41 \\ \hline \end{array}$ | 11. $\begin{array}{r} 31 \\ -\ 10 \\ \hline \end{array}$ | 12. $\begin{array}{r} 64 \\ -\ 24 \\ \hline \end{array}$ |

## Part 2

**Directions:** Solve the word problem below.

Shelby invited 34 people to her party. Before the party, 12 people told Shelby they could not come. How many people will be at Shelby's party?

**Show your work:**

**Answer:** _____

# Triple-Digit Subtraction in Action

## Part 1

**Directions:** Solve the triple-digit subtraction problems.

| | | | | | | | |
|---|---|---|---|---|---|---|---|
| 1. | 781 − 340 | 2. | 239 − 111 | 3. | 470 − 270 |

| 4. | 273 − 132 | 5. | 734 − 513 | 6. | 652 − 551 |
|---|---|---|---|---|---|

| 7. | 512 − 101 | 8. | 692 − 312 | 9. | 472 − 261 |
|---|---|---|---|---|---|

| 10. | 947 − 426 | 11. | 422 − 122 | 12. | 565 − 313 |
|---|---|---|---|---|---|

## Part 2

**Directions:** Solve the word problem below.

Pedro had 982 aluminum cans. He took 800 of the cans to the recycling center to be recycled. How many cans did Pedro have left?

**Show your work:**

**Answer:** _____

# Regroup to Subtract

Sometimes when you subtract, you need to regroup the numbers.

**Example:**

$$
\begin{array}{r}
2\;\nearrow 1 \text{ ten} \\
\cancel{3}2 \\
-\;27 \\
\hline
5
\end{array}
$$

**Directions:** Regroup, or borrow, as needed to solve each subtraction problem.

| | |
|---|---|
| 1. $\begin{array}{r} 36 \\ -\;19 \\ \hline \end{array}$ | 2. $\begin{array}{r} 84 \\ -\;55 \\ \hline \end{array}$ |
| 3. $\begin{array}{r} 76 \\ -\;48 \\ \hline \end{array}$ | 4. $\begin{array}{r} 33 \\ -\;17 \\ \hline \end{array}$ |
| 5. $\begin{array}{r} 58 \\ -\;29 \\ \hline \end{array}$ | 6. $\begin{array}{r} 28 \\ -\;9 \\ \hline \end{array}$ |
| 7. $\begin{array}{r} 22 \\ -\;19 \\ \hline \end{array}$ | 8. $\begin{array}{r} 57 \\ -\;39 \\ \hline \end{array}$ |
| 9. $\begin{array}{r} 42 \\ -\;26 \\ \hline \end{array}$ | 10. $\begin{array}{r} 24 \\ -\;15 \\ \hline \end{array}$ |

# Fun with Fact Families

A **math fact family** is a group of three numbers. When you add or subtract two numbers in the family, the answer is the third number.

**Directions:** Subtract and add each fact family to find the answers.

---

**1.**

$2 + 3 =$ _____

$5 - 3 =$ _____

**2.**

$6 + 4 =$ _____

$10 - 4 =$ _____

---

**3.**

$7 + 1 =$ _____

$8 - 1 =$ _____

**4.**

$4 + 4 =$ _____

$8 - 4 =$ _____

---

**5.**

$6 + 8 =$ _____

$14 - 8 =$ _____

**6.**

$9 + 8 =$ _____

$17 - 8 =$ _____

---

**7.**

$12 + 3 =$ _____

$15 - 3 =$ _____

**8.**

$7 + 5 =$ _____

$12 - 5 =$ _____

---

# Practice, Practice, Practice

**Directions:** Solve each problem.

If the problem is an addition problem, circle the **+** sign with a green crayon. If the problem is a subtraction problem, circle the **−** sign with a yellow crayon.

1.    $10 - 7 =$ _____        2.    $6 + 3 =$ _____

3.    $4 + 5 =$ _____        4.    $5 - 2 =$ _____

5.    $9 - 7 =$ _____        6.    $12 - 6 =$ _____

7.    $6 + 4 =$ _____        8.    $2 + 8 =$ _____

9.    $1 + 6 =$ _____        10.    $4 + 3 =$ _____

11.    $10 - 5 =$ _____        12.    $9 + 4 =$ _____

# Mixed Practice

**Directions:** Find the sum or difference.

| | | |
|---|---|---|
| **1.**       78<br>  − 14 | **2.**       22<br>  − 13 | **3.**       65<br>  − 24 |
| **4.**       65<br>  + 13 | **5.**       39<br>  − 18 | **6.**       82<br>  − 24 |
| **7.**       52<br>  − 31 | **8.**       24<br>  + 26 | **9.**       36<br>  + 13 |
| **10.**     98<br>  − 53 | **11.**     40<br>  + 20 | **12.**     84<br>  − 33 |
| **13.**     46<br>  + 16 | **14.**     91<br>  − 43 | **15.**     79<br>  + 10 |

# Understanding a Calendar

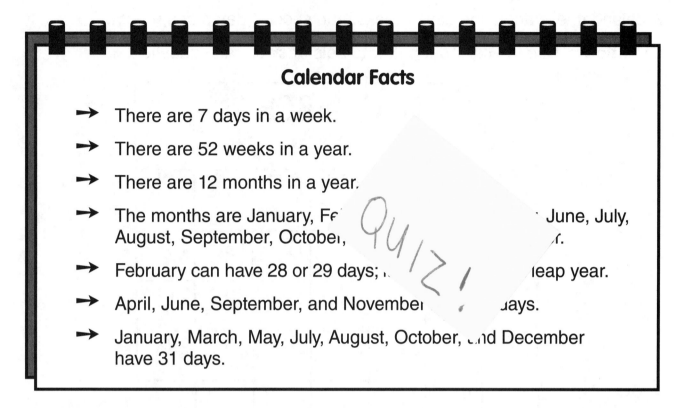

**Calendar Facts**

➡ There are 7 days in a week.

➡ There are 52 weeks in a year.

➡ There are 12 months in a year.

➡ The months are January, Fe[...] June, July,
August, September, October, [...].

➡ February can have 28 or 29 days; [...] leap year.

➡ April, June, September, and November [...] days.

➡ January, March, May, July, August, October, and December
have 31 days.

**Directions:** Circle the answer to each question. Write the correct answer on the
line and reread the sentence.

| 1. | _____ can have 28 or 29 days. | |
|---|---|---|
| | **a.** July | **b.** February |
| 2. | There are ____ days in a week. | |
| | **a.** 7 | **b.** 14 |
| 3. | There are ____ months in a year. | |
| | **a.** 6 | **b.** 12 |
| 4. | The first month of the year is _____. | |
| | **a.** January | **b.** December |
| 5. | _____ comes between March and May. | |
| | **a.** June | **b.** April |

# Using a Calendar

A calendar tells about the days, weeks, and specific dates of a month.

**Directions:** Use the calendar below to help answer each question.

## DECEMBER

| SUN | MON | TUE | WED | THURS | FRI | SAT |
|-----|-----|-----|-----|-------|-----|-----|
| 1 | 2 | 3 | 4 | 5 | 6 | 7 |
| 8 | 9 | 10 | 11 | 12 | 13 | 14 |
| 15 | 16 | 17 | 18 | 19 | 20 | 21 |
| 22 | 23 | 24 | 25 | 26 | 27 | 28 |
| 29 | 30 | 31 | | | | |

1. How many days are there in a week? _____

2. According to the calendar, what is the first day of the week?_____

3. Which day of the week is December 4?_____

4. December 5 comes between which two dates? _____

   and _____

5. Which day of the week is the last day of the month?_____

6. How many Saturdays are in the month of December?_____

7. On which day of the week does December start? _____

# Estimating Time

**Time Facts**
- There are 60 seconds in 1 minute.
- There are 60 minutes in 1 hour.
- There are 24 hours in 1 day.

**Directions:** Estimate how long it will take to do each task. Circle the correct answer.

| | |
|---|---|
| **1.** About how long will it take to comb your hair? | |
| **a.** 4 minutes | **b.** 4 hours |
| **2.** About how long did it take for you to work problem number 1? | |
| **a.** 10 seconds | **b.** 10 hours |
| **3.** About how long will it take to eat lunch? | |
| **a.** about 30 minutes | **b.** about 20 seconds |
| **4.** About how much sleep do you need each night? | |
| **a.** about 10 minutes | **b.** about 10 hours |
| **5.** About how long does it take you to write a sentence? | |
| **a.** about 3 minutes | **b.** about 3 hours |
| **6.** About how long does it take you to complete a full day of school? | |
| **a.** about 7 minutes | **b.** about 7 hours |

# Learning to Tell Time

**Directions:** Write the time shown on each clock.

| | |
|---|---|
| 1.  _____ | 2.  _____ |
| 3.  _____ | 4.  _____ |
| 5.  _____ | 6.  _____ |
| 7.  _____ | 8.  _____ |

# Different Clocks

Some clocks have an hour hand and a minute hand. These clocks are called **analog** clocks. **Digital** clocks use numbers to show digital time.

**Directions:** Read the time on each analog clock. Then write the time on the digital clock beside it.

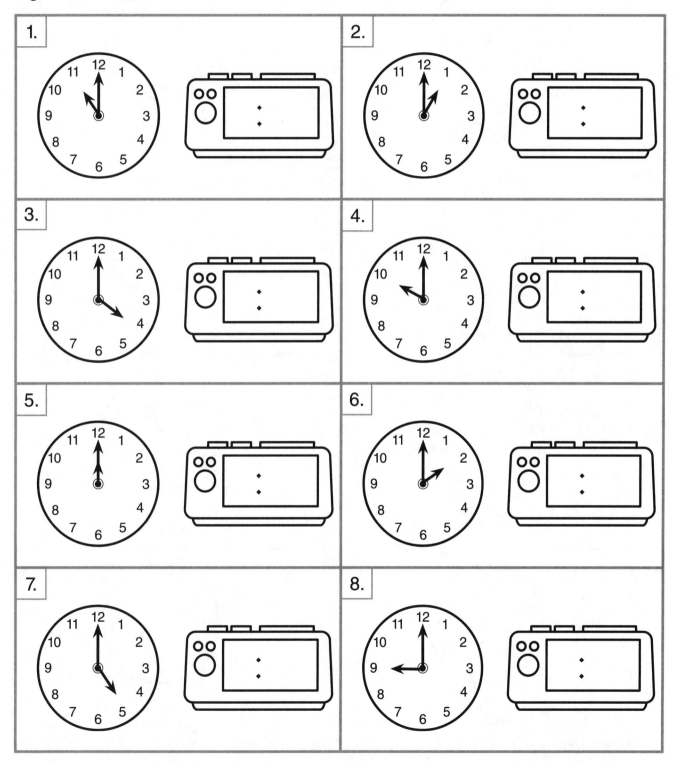

# w the Time

**Directions:** d the minute hand on each analog clock to show the tim

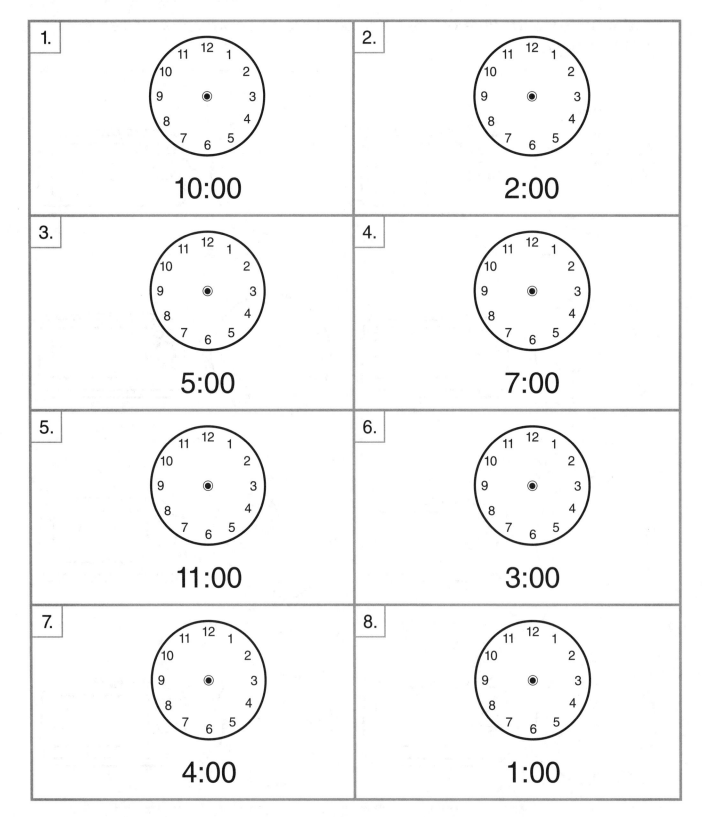

1. 10:00

2. 2:00

3. 5:00

4. 7:00

5. 11:00

6. 3:00

7. 4:00

8. 1:00

# More About Time

Time can be read in different ways. You can say four-thirty.
You can say half past four. You can say 30 minutes after four.
Each way is correct.

**Directions:** Draw the hands on the clock to show the time that is given.

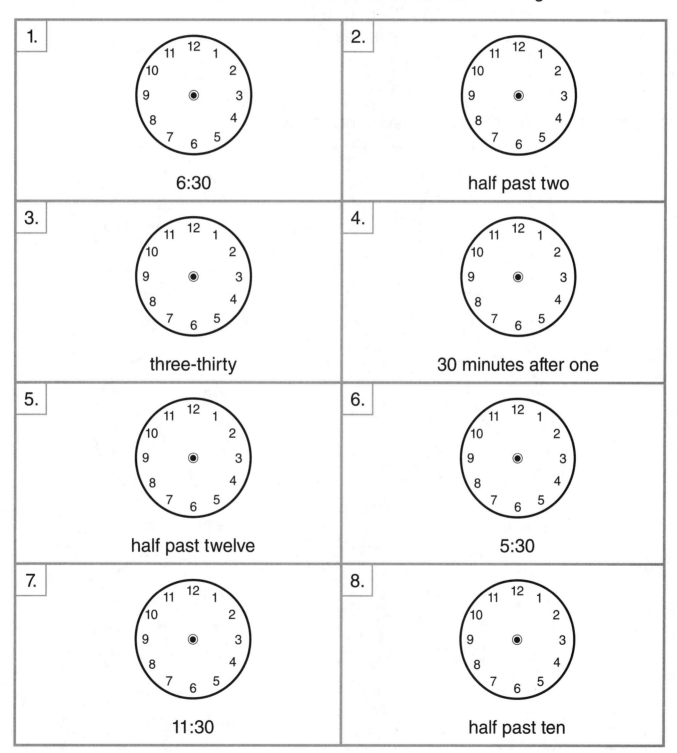

| | |
|---|---|
| 1.  6:30 | 2.  half past two |
| 3.  three-thirty | 4.  30 minutes after one |
| 5.  half past twelve | 6.  5:30 |
| 7.  11:30 | 8.  half past ten |

# Count by 5s to Help Tell Time

Counting by 5s helps you tell time. You can count by 5s to count the minutes after the hour.

**Example**

The time is 8:25. Count by 5s to show how many minutes there are past 8:00.

**Directions:** Write the time that each clock shows.

1.

The time is 7: _____

2.

The time is 12: _____

3.

The time is 8: _____

4.

The time is 6: _____

5.

The time is 5: _____

6.

The time is 10: _____

# Math and Money

|  |  |  |  |
|---|---|---|---|
| a penny = 1¢ | a nickel = 5¢ | a dime = 10¢ | a quarter = 25¢ |

**Directions:** Add each set of coins to find the total. Write the amount on the line.

1. = _____

2. = _____

3. = _____

4. = _____

5. = _____

6. = _____

7. = _____

8. = _____

# Buying Power

**Directions:** Color the set of coins that shows the price of each item.

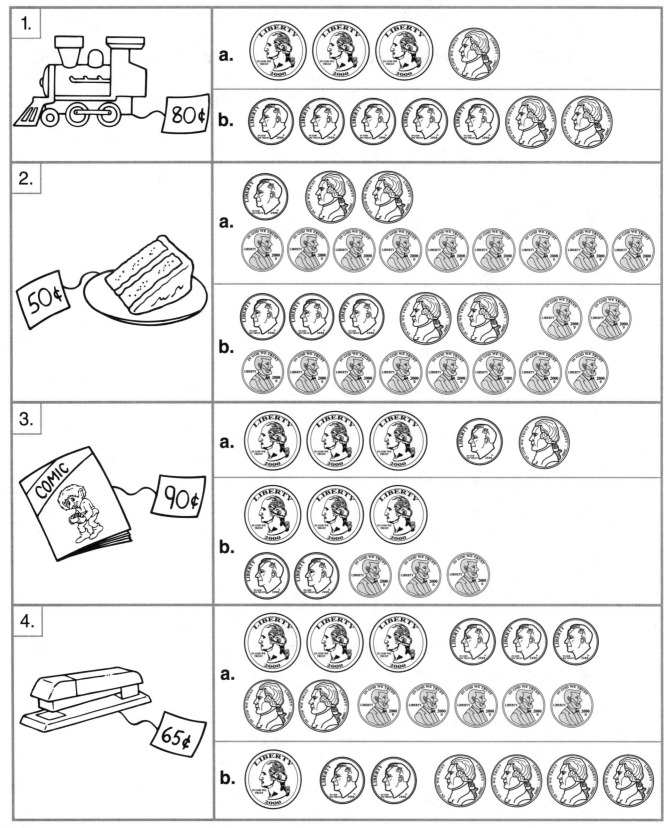

# Greater or Less Than
# with Money Amounts

**Directions:** Add the coins in each group. Use the greater than **>** or less than **<** sign to compare money.

1.

2.

3.

4.

5.

6.

# Making Change

At a store, each item for sale will have a price on it. When someone wants to buy the item, he might pay cash for it. If you give the cashier more money than the item costs, you will get change back.

**Example:**

**Cost:** $1.50        **Money given to cashier:** $2.00

$$\begin{array}{r} \$2.00 \\ -\$1.50 \\ \hline \$0.50 \end{array}$$

**Directions:** Subtract to find each answer.

| 1. | Samantha had $7.50. She bought a package of stickers for $2.50. How much money did Samantha have once she bought the stickers? |

**Show your work:**



**Answer:** $ _____

| 2. | The cost of a movie ticket was $6.00. Gage had $10.00. He bought one ticket. How much change did Gage get back after buying one movie ticket? |

**Show your work:**



**Answer:** $ _____

| 3. | Carlotta wants to buy a toy at the store. The toy costs $12.50. Carlotta has $20.00. If Carlotta buys the toy, how much money will she have left? |

**Show your work:**



**Answer:** $ _____

# Learning Measurement

An **inch** is a small unit of measurement.  An inch is this long: _____

This piece of string is also an inch long.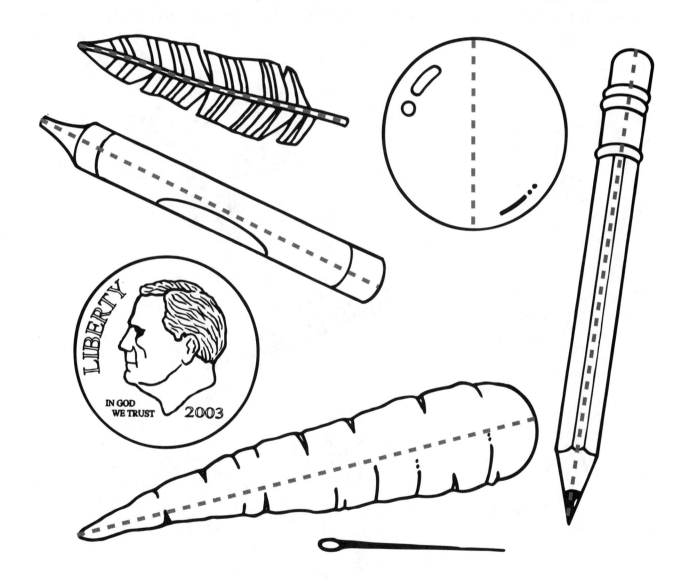

A ruler is usually 12 inches long.  **12 inches = 1 foot**

**Directions:** Use a ruler to measure each object.

1. Circle the 2-inch objects.
2. Draw a box around the 3-inch object.
3. Color the 5-inch objects orange.
4. Color the 4-inch object green.

**Something Extra:** On the back of this page, draw something that would be 12 inches, or one foot long.

# Another Way to Measure

You can measure the length of things by measuring in centimeters.

A **centimeter** is a metric measurement. This line is 1 centimeter: ▬

10 centimeters is called a **decimeter.**

▬▬▬▬▬▬▬▬▬▬▬

**Directions:** Cut out the centimeter ruler at the bottom of the page. Use it to measure the length of each item. Write the measurements on the lines.

1. _____ feather

2. _____ bug

3. _____ worm

4. _____ gum

5. _____ circle

6. _____ ribbon

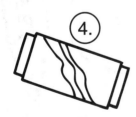

**Centimeter Ruler**

| 1 2 3 4 5 6 7 8 9 10 11 12 |

# What Does It Weigh?

A **pound** is one unit of measurement for weight.

Here are some things that weigh about a pound.

**Directions:** Circle the objects that would weigh *more* than a pound. Color the objects that weigh *less* than a pound.

**Something Extra:** On the back of this paper, draw a picture of something that weighs about one pound.

# Cold and Hot Stuff

A **thermometer** is used to measure temperature. A thermometer tells how cold or how hot something is.

**Directions:** Use a red crayon to color the inside of each thermometer so it will match the temperature given.

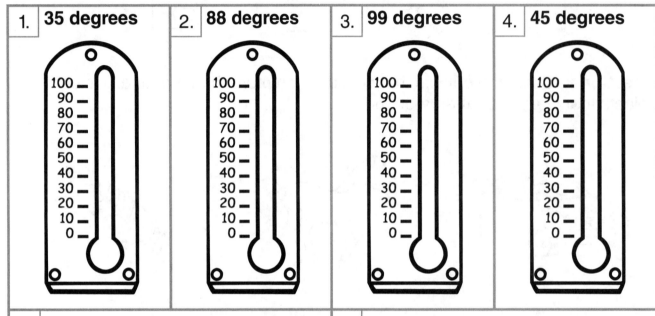

1. **35 degrees**
2. **88 degrees**
3. **99 degrees**
4. **45 degrees**

5. Amy needs to freeze her ice cream. She wants the freezer temperature to be set at 30 degrees. Color the thermometer to show 30 degrees.

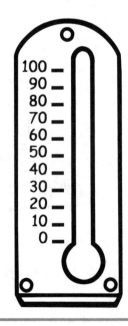

6. Sam wants to fly his kite. The weather is windy. The temperature outside is 72 degrees. It is a perfect day for flying his kite. Color the thermometer to show 72 degrees.

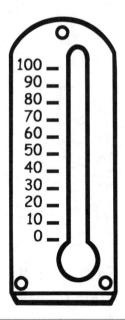

# A Fraction or a Part

A **fraction** is a section or part of something.

This circle is divided into six sections or parts.

If someone gives you one section of this circle, you will get 1/6 of the circle. 1/6 is a fraction, or a part of the circle.

$\frac{1}{6}$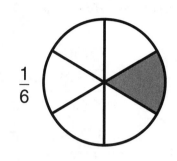

**Directions:** Color the picture to show the fraction.

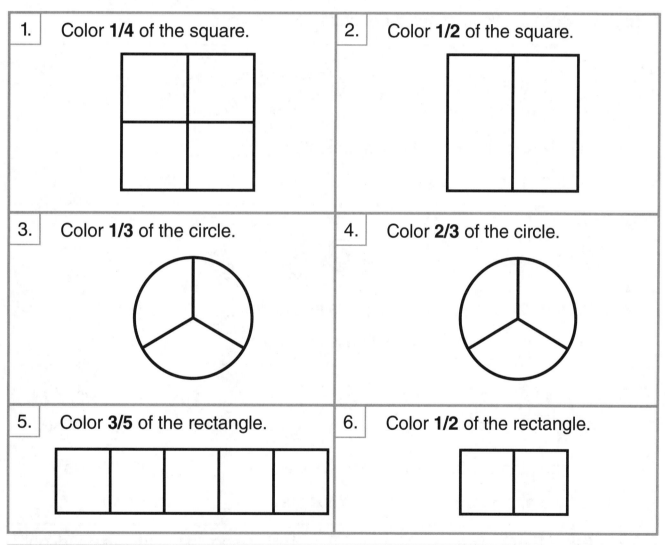

1. Color **1/4** of the square.

2. Color **1/2** of the square.

3. Color **1/3** of the circle.

4. Color **2/3** of the circle.

5. Color **3/5** of the rectangle.

6. Color **1/2** of the rectangle.

**Something Extra:** Draw a square. Divide the square into four equal parts. Color **3/4** of the square.

# More with Fractions

When you have a group with mixed items, you can describe the items as fractions.

**Example**

These items can be read as two different fractions.

2/3 of the group is apples.

1/3 of the group is a strawberry.

**Directions:** Write two fractions for each group of items.

**1.**

Of all the animals, what fraction are cats? _____ cats

Of all the animals, what fraction are dogs? _____ dogs

**2.**

Of all the ice cream, what fraction is in a bowl? _____ bowls

Of all the ice cream, what fraction is in a cone? _____ cones

**3.**

Of all the plants, what fraction has no flowers? _____ no flowers

Of all the plants, what fraction has flowers? _____ with flowers

**Something Extra:** Draw six shapes. Two shapes should be squares and four of the shapes should be triangles. Write the fraction of squares and triangles on the lines.

_____ squares

_____ triangles

# Plane Shapes

The shapes below are known as plane shapes.

**Directions:** Follow the directions for each group of plane shapes.

| | |
|---|---|
| 1. | Color triangles blue.  Color trapezoids yellow.  Color parallelograms orange. |

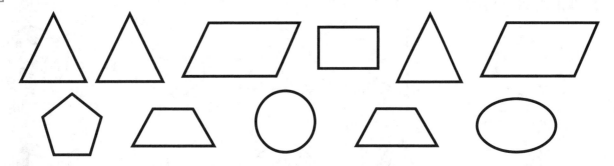

| | |
|---|---|
| 2. | Color squares red.  Color circles green.  Color rectangles blue.  Color hexagons yellow. |

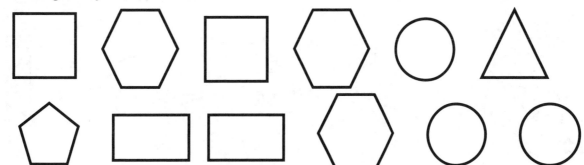

| | |
|---|---|
| 3. | Draw X's on the hexagons.  Draw hearts on the triangles.  Draw stars on the parallelograms. |

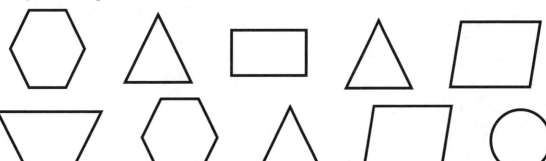

# Learning About Solid Figures

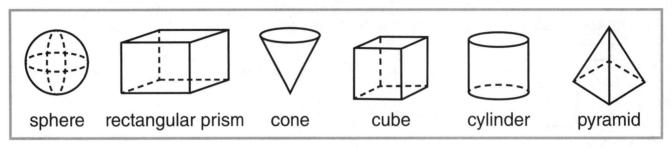

sphere    rectangular prism    cone    cube    cylinder    pyramid

## Part 1

**Directions:** Follow the directions for each problem.

1. Color all pyramids blue.

2. Color all cones orange.

3. Color all cylinders red.

## Part 2

**Directions:** Draw a line to match each shape to its name.

1.                 **rectangular prism**

2.                 **sphere**

3.                 **cube**

# Shapes That Are Congruent

Shapes or figures that are the same shape and size are **congruent**.

> **Example**
>
> These triangles are congruent.

**Directions:** Circle **yes** if the figures are congruent. Circle **no** if the figures are not congruent.

| 1. | | 2. | |
|---|---|---|---|
| **a.** yes <br> **b.** no | | **a.** yes <br> **b.** no | |
| 3. | | 4. | |
| **a.** yes <br> **b.** no | | **a.** yes <br> **b.** no | |
| 5. | | 6. | |
| **a.** yes <br> **b.** no | | **a.** yes <br> **b.** no | |
| 7. | | 8. | |
| **a.** yes <br> **b.** no | | **a.** yes <br> **b.** no | |

# And So It Goes

**Directions:** Find the pattern. Then draw an **X** on the mistake in the pattern. Explain your answer.

---

**1.**

This **AB** pattern is a mistake because _____

_____

---

**2.**

This **AB** pattern is a mistake because _____

_____

---

**3.**

This **ABC** pattern is a mistake because _____

_____

---

**4.**

1, 2, 3, A, B, C, 4, 5, 6, D, E, F, 7, 9, 9, G, H, I

This **ABC** pattern is a mistake because _____

_____

# Perfect Patterns

**Directions:** Figure out each pattern. Then draw inside each blank shape to continue the pattern.

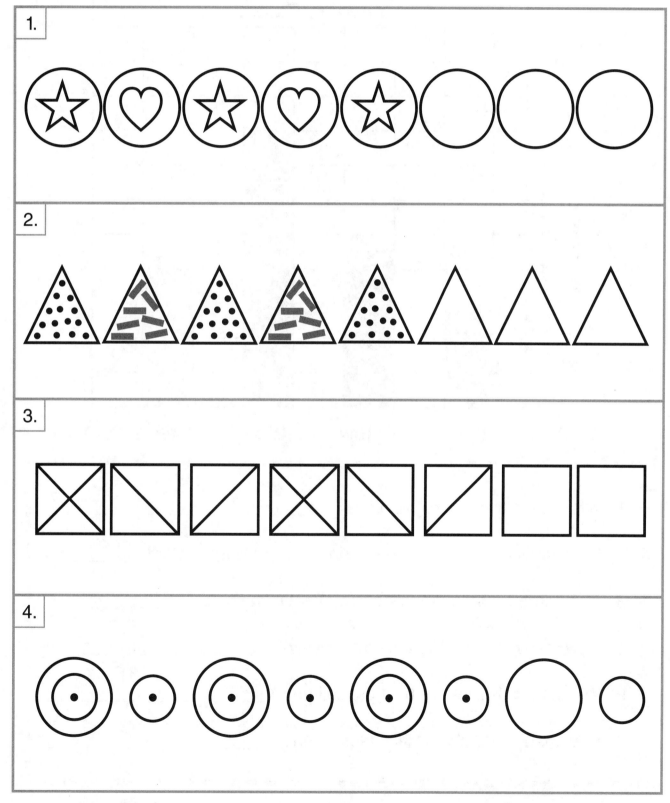

# Reading a Graph

**Directions:** Use the graph to help answer each question.

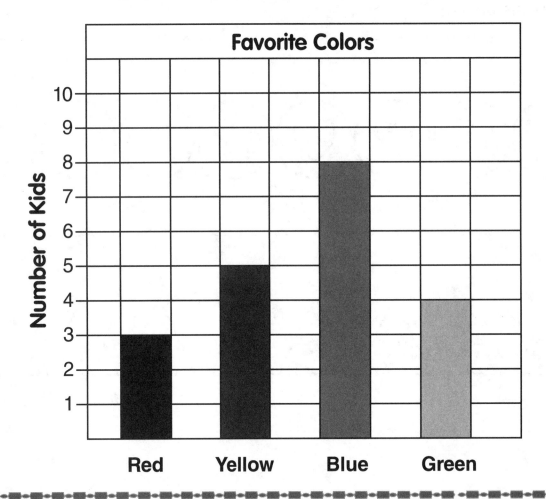

1.  What is the title of the graph? _____

2.  How many children were asked about their favorite color? _____

3.  Only three children like this color.  What is the color? _____

4.  How many children like the color yellow? _____

5.  Which color is liked by the most children? _____

6.  How many children like the color green? _____

# Understanding a Line Graph

**Directions:** Use the line graph below to answer the questions.

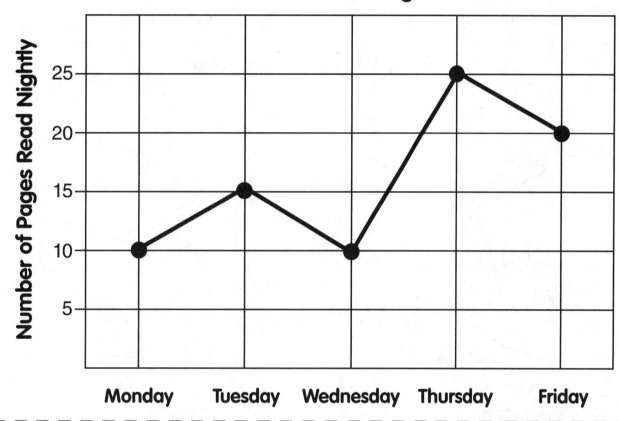

**Kate's School Reading Journal**

1. What is the title of the graph? _____

    _____

2. What do the numbers on the left of the graph show? _____

    _____

3. On which day did Kate read the most pages of her book? _____

    _____

4. On which days did Kate read the fewest pages of her book? _____

    _____

5. How many total pages did Kate read during the school week? _____

    _____

# Beginning Map Skills

Maps are made up of many parts. One important part of a map is the map key. A **map key** shows you how to read the symbols that are on a map. It tells you what each symbol on the map means.

**Directions:** Look at the map. Use the map key to answer the questions.

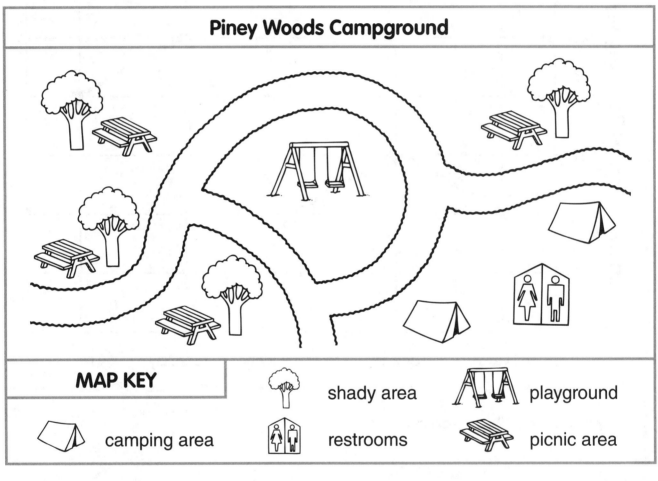

1. What is the title of the map? _____

   _____

2. Why does a map need a map key? _____

   _____

3. How many tent camping areas are there for campers? _____

4. How many picnic areas are shaded? _____

5. What does the symbol [image] mean? _____

# Learning the World

**Directions:** Use the map below to help complete the activity.

_____

**Map Title**

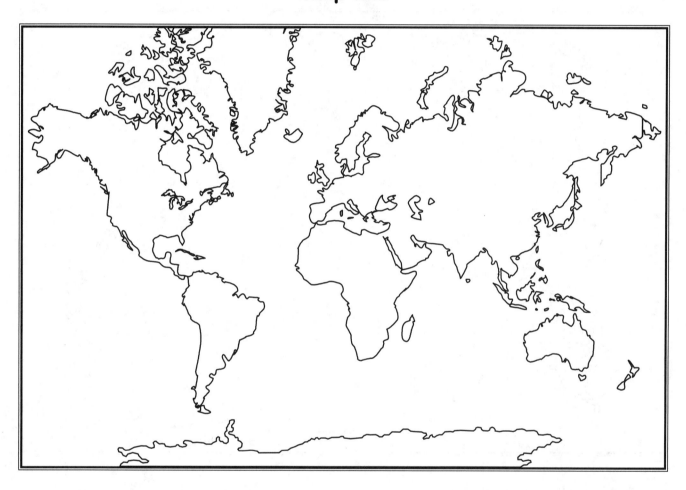

1. Label the seven continents on the map: **North America, South America, Europe, Asia, Africa, Australia,** and **Antarctica**.

2. Color Australia orange.

3. Find the Pacific Ocean. Write the word *Pacific* in this area.

4. Give this map a title. Write it on the line above the map.

5. Color Africa green.

6. Find the Atlantic Ocean. Write the word *Atlantic* in this area.

# All Around the World

**Directions:** Look at the map of the world. Use the map to help answer the questions that follow.

**Note:** Some of the animals can live in other parts of the world, but use only what is given on the map to answer your questions.

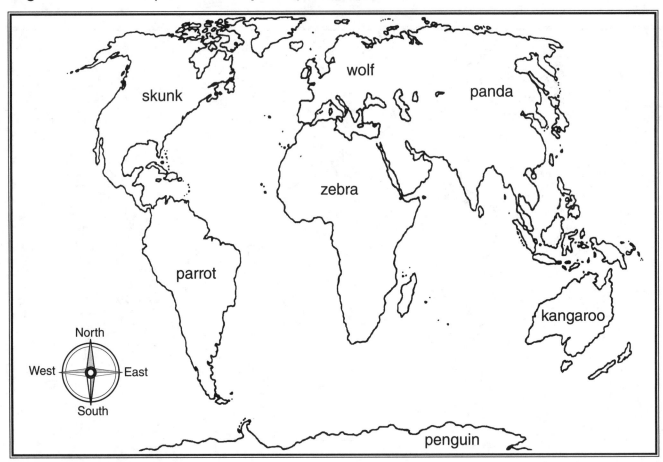

1. Skunks live on this continent:_____

2. Australia is located_____ of Asia.

3. According to the map, penguins live on which continent? _____

4. The panda bear lives in which direction from the kangaroo?_____

5. On which continent can you find wolves? _____

6. According to the map, where do parrots live? _____

# A Compass Rose

A **compass rose** is used to tell directions on a map. The cardinal directions or cardinal points are **north**, **south**, **east**, and **west**.

**Directions:** Fill in the cardinal directions on the compass rose. Color the compass rose when you are finished.

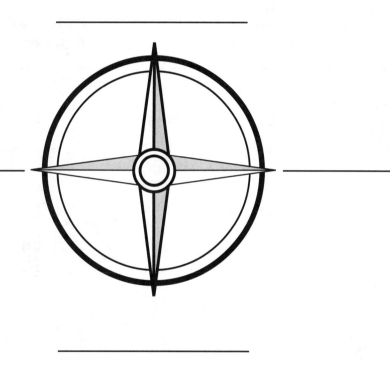

**Something Extra:** Give one reason why a map should have a compass rose.

_____

_____

_____

# Using a Compass Rose

A **compass rose** shows the cardinal directions or points: **north**, **south**, **west**, and **east**.

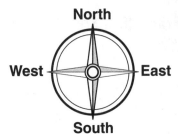

**Directions:** Look at the map below and use the compass rose to help answer the questions. Answer each question with one or more cardinal directions.

1. Which direction are the swings from the slide? _____

2. Which direction are the monkey bars from the jungle gym? _____

3. Which direction is the school's entrance from the fountain? _____

4. You are sitting at the picnic area. Which directions would you need to travel to get to the swings? _____

5. If you were at the slide and wanted to go to the jungle gym, which directions would you need to go?_____

# Reading a Map

**Directions:** Use the map to answer each question.

1. Color Canada yellow.

2. Color the United States of America red.

3. Color Mexico green.

4. Which two oceans border North America?

_____     _____

5. Which country is between Canada and Mexico?

_____

# A Map and a Globe

**Directions:** Use the pictures to help you answer the questions. Circle the correct answer(s) for each question. Write the answers on the lines provided.

 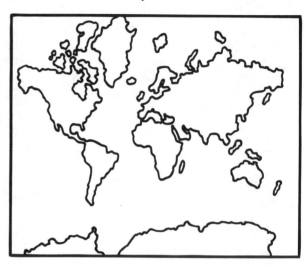

1. A globe is a map of the world that is shaped like a _____ .

   **a.** sphere                    **b.** square

2. A globe and a map both show pictures of _____ .

   **a.** landforms                 **b.** houses

3. If you are looking at a globe, it shows _____ .

   **a.** one half of the world     **b.** all of the world at once

4. A map can show the entire world at once because it is _____ .

   **a.** shaped like a sphere      **b.** flat

5. The imaginary line that separates the world into two parts is _____ .

   **a.** the signal                **b.** the equator

6. You could find a _____ in a book, but you could not find a _____ .

   **a.** map, globe                **b.** globe, map

# Map Review

## Part 1

**Directions:** Use the Word Bank to help answer the questions.

| Word Bank | | |
|---|---|---|
| compass rose | oceans | continents |
| map key | globe | equator |

1. A model of the Earth shaped like a sphere is called a _____.

2. The _____ shows the cardinal directions on a map.

3. The _____ explains the symbols on a map.

4. An imaginary line that divides the Earth in half is the _____.

5. The largest bodies of land are called _____.

6. The_____ are the largest bodies of water on Earth.

## Part 2

**Directions:** A globe shows the seven continents of the world.  Use a globe to find the names of the seven continents.  List them in the space below.

### The Seven Continents

_____        _____

_____        _____

_____        _____

_____

# Learning About the Past

**History** is the story of everything that has happened in the past. It tells about the people who lived and events that happened in an earlier time.

**Directions:** Circle the correct definition for each word.

1. Something found that was made by people from the past is _____ .

    **a.** an artifact

    **b.** an archaeologist

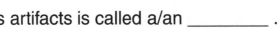

2. Someone who studies artifacts is called a/an _____ .

    **a.** geologist

    **b.** archaeologist

3. Early communities where people gathered to live were often called _____ .

    **a.** settlements

    **b.** pioneers

4. What is known about the past is called _____ .

    **a.** history

    **b.** modern times

5. A graph that shows events and times of the past might be a _____ .

    **a.** time line

    **b.** timepiece

6. One important tool for keeping track of time is a _____ .

    **a.** calculator

    **b.** calendar

# Understanding a Time Line

A **time line** shows the order in which events occurred.  Placing events in order by time is called chronological order.

**Directions:**  Use the time line to answer the questions that follow.

## Important American Historical Events

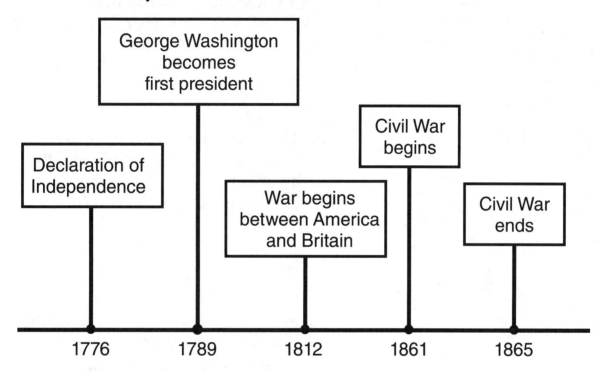

1.  In what year did George Washington become president? _____

2.  According to the time line, which happened first:  the Civil War or the War of 1812? _____

3.  What happened in the year 1865? _____

4.  Who fought against America in the War of 1812? _____

5.  In what year was the Declaration of Independence signed? _____

6.  What happened first:  the signing of the Declaration of Independence or George Washington becoming president? _____

_____

# Important American Monuments and Symbols

**Directions:** Draw a line to match each picture to its description.

1.

   **a.** This famous bell in Philadelphia, Pennsylvania, is a symbol of freedom and the Revolutionary War.

2.

   **b.** This symbol has 13 stripes and 50 stars. The stripes stand for the 13 colonies. The stars stand for the 50 states.

3.

   **c.** Independence Hall in Pennsylvania is where the Declaration of Independence was signed.

4.

   **d.** This bird is an important symbol of the United States of America.

5.

   **e.** This is a document that told England the colonists wanted to be free.

# The Earliest Americans

The earliest Americans are known as Indians. The Indians did not use this name. Christopher Columbus landed in the Americas in 1492. Columbus thought he had landed in India. He called the people he met Indians. The Indians called themselves by their tribal names.

There were many tribes in the Americas. No one knows exactly how the Indians came to be in the Americas. There are many different theories or ideas. Some people think there may have once been a land bridge connecting the continents. Some people believe the Indians may have walked across this land bridge from Asia while following herds of animals.

Just as you do not live exactly like people in other towns or cities, Indians did not all live in the same ways. Some Indians settled and farmed the lands around them. Other Indians did not settle but traveled across the land in search of food. No matter how they lived, the Indians all respected the land. They used only what they needed and took care of Earth.

**Directions:** Use the paragraphs above to answer the questions.

1. Who were the earliest known Americans?_____

2. Why did Christopher Columbus call the natives "Indians"? _____

   _____

3. How do some people think the Indians came to be in the Americas?

   _____

4. Were some Indians farmers?_____

5. Why did some Indians travel across the land?_____

   _____

6. All tribes are known for taking care of _____ .

# The Early Colonists

The original United States began from 13 colonies. The people who lived in these colonies were not free. The colonies belonged to England. Many of the people who lived in the colonies were from England.

People came to live in the colonies for many reasons. Some came for religious freedom. Some came to own their own land. Some came for the chance to make money. The people who came to live in the colonies began to see themselves more as Americans and less as English citizens. They wanted to have a voice in their government. They wanted to decide their own laws. They could not do any of this because the colonies were owned by England's king. The colonists would eventually begin a war for independence known as the Revolutionary War.

**Directions:** Use the paragraphs above to answer the questions.

1. The people who lived in the original 13 colonies were not_____ .

2. The 13 colonies actually belonged to the King of_____ .

3. Many of the original settlers of the 13 colonies were from which country?

   _____

4. List two reasons why people came to live in the colonies:

   _____

   _____ .

5. The colonists wanted to have a _____ in their government.

6. The war for independence was called the _____

   _____ .

# Know the Vocabulary

A good citizen knows about the community he or she lives in and wants to make the community a better place. People often do this by being involved in their system of government.

Learn the important vocabulary words below that will help make you a better citizen!

**Directions:** Choose the correct definition for each word. Circle your choice.

1. **government**

    **a.** a group of people who are on television

    **b.** a group of people who make rules and laws

2. **taxes**

    **a.** money people pay to go on vacation

    **b.** money people pay to the government

3. **volunteer**

    **a.** someone who gets paid to do a job

    **b.** someone who offers to help

4. **law**

    **a.** a rule that everyone must follow

    **b.** a rule that people decide not to follow

5. **vote**

    **a.** a choice that is counted

    **b.** a rule or law

6. **freedom**

    **a.** having the right to make decisions

    **b.** being told what to do

# Understanding the Government

In the United States of America, every community has some type of government. A **government** is an organized group of people who make the rules and laws people must follow. There are local, state, and national governments that help make our rules and laws. Citizens get to vote in an election and decide who their leaders will be. This is important because these leaders protect the rights and freedoms of the people they represent.

**Directions:** Use the paragraph above to answer each question.

1. Every community has some type of _____.

2. A government is a group that makes the rules and _____ that people must follow.

3. What are the three levels of government? _____, _____, and _____

4. Who gets to vote in an election? _____

5. In an election, the people decide who their _____ will be.

6. Leaders protect the _____ and _____ of the people they represent.

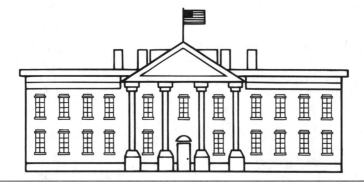

**Something Extra:** Who is the leader of your state? This person is called the governor.

The governor of my state is _____.

He/she is governor of the state of_____.

# Good Community Helpers

**Directions:** Look at the poster below and answer the questions.

## A Recycling Fair!

Come to the Recycling Fair on **Saturday, August 8**.

**8:00 – 12:00 noon** at Eastside Elementary

Bring your newspapers and aluminum cans.

- All the money raised will go to help Eastside Elementary get new playground equipment.

- Clean up around your house by getting rid of those piles of cans and stacks of newspapers.

- Free lemonade will be provided.

- Volunteers are needed to help run the fair. Call Eastside Elementary if you want to volunteer.

1. Why is the school having this fair? _____

_____

2. Why would people who go to this fair be examples of good citizens?

_____

3. Where is the fair being held? _____

4. What is being bought with any money that is raised?

_____

5. Which two items are being collected for recycling?

_____

# It's Important to Vote

It is important to vote when you are a citizen. When you vote, your opinion counts. People vote to make decisions in their government. People also vote for many other things. Voting is an important responsibility that people have.

**Directions:** Read the paragraph and look at the graph below to answer the questions.

## The School Field Trip

Mrs. Winters' class is going on a field trip. The students voted to see where they will go on their trip. The students voted to go to either the zoo or to the movie theater.

Mrs. Winters gave each student a ticket. On the ticket were the words *zoo* and *movie*. Each student circled his or her choice to show their vote.

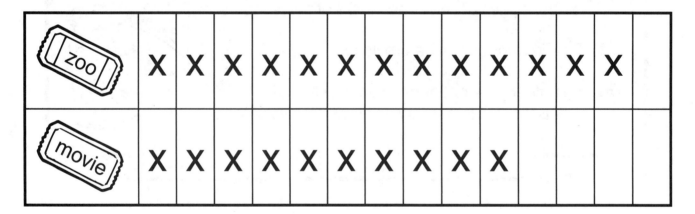

| | | | | | | | | | | | | | |
|---|---|---|---|---|---|---|---|---|---|---|---|---|---|
| zoo | X | X | X | X | X | X | X | X | X | X | X | X | X |
| movie | X | X | X | X | X | X | X | X | X | X | | | |

1. How many total students voted on the field trip? _____

2. How many students voted to go to the zoo? _____

3. How many students voted to go to the movie? _____

4. Which field trip event will the students be attending?_____

5. Give two reasons why it was a good idea for Mrs. Winters to let the class vote on where they would go for their field trip.

   **a.** _____

   **b.** _____

# The Flag

Citizens can say the pledge to the flag.  The flag of the United States of America has many special symbols.  Its 13 stripes stand for the original 13 colonies.  The colonies won their independence from England during the Revolutionary War.  The 50 stars on the flag stand for the 50 states in the United States.  The colors of the flag are red, white, and blue.  Many students start their school day pledging to the flag.

**Directions:**  Color the flag.  Then answer the questions that follow.

1. How many stripes are on the flag? _____

2. What do the stripes represent or stand for?_____

   _____

3. What do the stars on the flag stand for? _____

   _____

4. How many stars are on the flag? _____

5. What colors are on the flag? _____

   _____

# Name Those Parts

**Directions:** Use the Word Bank below to help label the parts of the plant. Color the picture when you are finished.

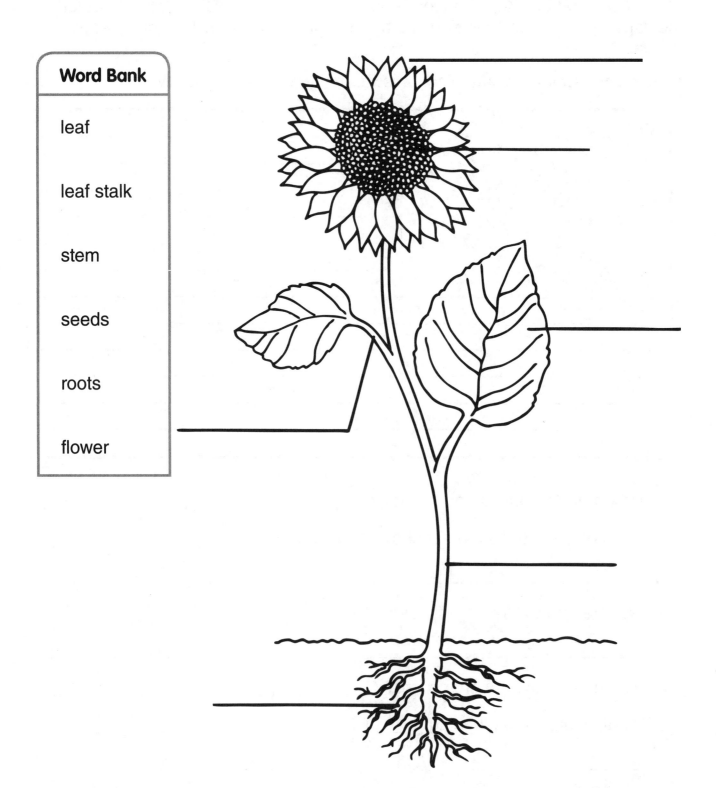

**Word Bank**

leaf

leaf stalk

stem

seeds

roots

flower

# What Plants Need

**Directions:** Think about what most plants need to survive. Look at the plants below. Color only the pictures on the pots that plants need in order to grow.

# Plants We Use

Plants are important to people for more than just oxygen. People use plants in many different ways. Complete the sentences below to see some special ways people use plants. Use reference materials to help you answer the questions.

**Directions:** Circle the correct answer and write it on the line provided.

1. People use the cotton plant to make _____ .

   **a.** material for clothes      **b.** lumber for houses

2. People use tomatoes to make many foods, including _____ .

   **a.** ketchup          **b.** sugar

3. Many plants were used by Native Americans to help make_____ .

   **a.** medicines        **b.** computers

4. A garden is a group of plants that are grown for people _____ .

   **a.** to throw away      **b.** to eat

---

**Something Extra:** In the space below, draw a picture of your favorite plant. Then explain why the plant is your favorite.




This plant is my favorite because _____

_____ .

---

# The Four Main Groups

Animals are divided into four main groups: *mammals, amphibians, reptiles,* and *birds*.

**Directions:** Color only the animals in each section that match the heading.

**Mammals**                              **Amphibians**

**Reptiles**                                **Birds**

# About Animals

Animals live in many different areas. The place an animal lives is called its **habitat**.

Animals that are hunted by other animals are called **prey**.

Animals that are the hunters are called **predators**. Animals often choose their habitat based on where their prey lives.

**Directions:** Circle the correct answer.

1. A fish would likely live in this habitat.

    **a.** the woods

    **b.** river

2. An animal that is a predator of fish is a _____ .

    **a.** bear

    **b.** worm

3. _____ are the prey of many fish.

    **a.** Insects

    **b.** Ducks

4. A river might also be a habitat for what other animal?

    **a.** dog

    **b.** turtle

---

**Something Extra:** Draw a habitat with a creek or river running through it. Show at least three animals that would do well in this habitat.

# Types of Clouds

**Directions:** Draw a picture in each box of the type of cloud that is described.

**Cirrus** are high, thin clouds. They are white and made out of tiny ice pieces.

**Stratus** are low, flat, gray clouds. They are usually in layers.

**Cumulus** are white, puffy clouds. They are often seen on sunny days.

**Nimbus** are puffy storm clouds. They are usually dark gray or black.

# Changing Seasons

What causes the seasons?  The seasons are caused by Earth revolving around the sun.  When Earth revolves around the sun, it moves on its **orbit** or path.  It takes Earth 365 days to **orbit** the sun.  A year is 365 days.  So, it takes Earth one year to orbit the sun.  When Earth orbits the sun, it causes different sections of Earth to tilt or face the sun.  This change is what causes the seasons on Earth.  When Earth is tilted closer to the sun, people on Earth have warmer weather.  When Earth is farther from the sun, Earth has cooler weather.

Places on Earth that are near the equator stay warm because the position of the sun stays the same for them.  The equator is the imaginary line that separates the planet into two equal parts— north and south.

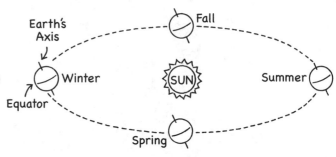

**Directions:** Use the paragraphs above to answer the questions.

1. The seasons are caused by Earth revolving around the _____ .

2. How many days does it take Earth to orbit the sun? _____ .

3. How many years does it take Earth to orbit the sun? _____ .

4. As Earth tilts toward and away from the sun, people on Earth have different

   _____ .

5. The warmer seasons happen when Earth is tilted _____ the sun.

6. The cooler seasons happen when Earth is tilted_____ from the sun.

7. The imaginary line that separates Earth into two parts is called

   the _____ .

8. The weather near the equator is usually _____ and not cold.

# The Amazing Water Cycle

Earth's water cycle is amazing. It goes in an endless cycle. The three parts of the water cycle are **evaporation, condensation,** and **precipitation**.

**Directions:** Look at the picture below to better understand the water cycle. Use the Word Bank to help label each part of the cycle.

| Word Bank | | |
|---|---|---|
| condensation | precipitation | evaporation |

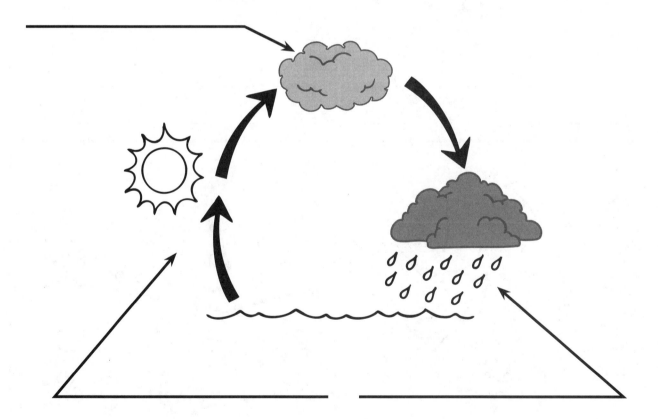

**Something Extra:** On the back of this sheet, write about a day that had lots of precipitation. Describe how you had fun that day, or why it was not fun.

# Weather Pictures

**Directions:** Look at each weather picture. Describe the weather in each picture. Color each picture when you are finished.

# Is It Going to Be a Rainy Day?

**Directions:** Use the weather map below to help answer the questions.

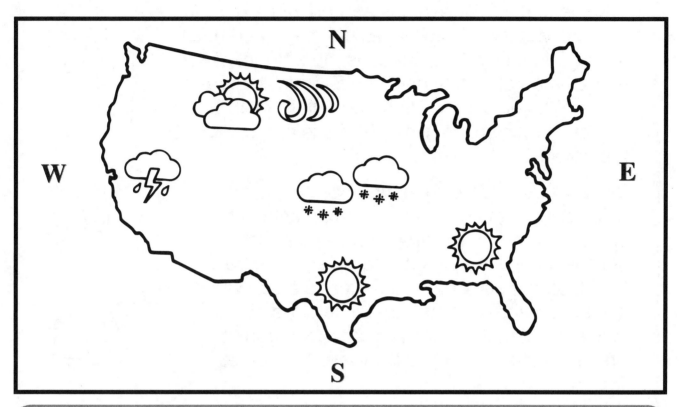

| sunny | cloudy | windy | snow | rainstorm |

1. This weather map is for which country? _____

2. What is the weather going to be like in the South? _____

3. Will people in the Midwest need to wear coats and gloves? _____
   Why or why not? _____

4. Which section of the country is expecting storms? _____

5. What is the weather going to be like where you live? _____

   _____

   How do you know?_____

   _____

# All That Matters

What is matter?  The things around you are made of matter.  **Matter** takes up space and has mass.  What is mass?  **Mass** is the amount of matter in an object.  Gravity on Earth gives the mass of an object its weight.  But, if that same object were in space, where there is no gravity, the object would lose its mass.

Matter is usually found in three forms:  a solid, a liquid, or a gas.  Some matter can actually change forms.  For example, water can be a solid when it is frozen into ice.  Water can be a liquid, of course.  And, water can be a gas when it is boiled and then evaporates into the air. However, some matter never changes from its original state but instead is always the same.

**Directions:** Circle the correct answer and write it on the line provided.

| | |
|---|---|
| 1. | All things are made up of_____. |
| | **a.** mass                              **b.** matter |
| 2. | All matter takes up _____. |
| | **a.** space and has mass        **b.** time and has mass |
| 3. | Gravity gives the mass of an object its _____. |
| | **a.** matter                            **b.** weight |
| 4. | Matter is usually found in these three forms: _____. |
| | **a.** solid, liquid, and gas      **b.** solid, round, and melted |

# Knowing the States of Matter

When matter is in a **liquid** form, it can take the shape of whatever it is poured into. Think about what happens to milk when you pour it into a glass. The milk takes the shape of the glass.

When matter has a shape of its own, it is a **solid**. A pencil or a tree is an example of matter that is solid.

When matter is a **gas**, it can also spread out to fill a container. Matter that is a gas does not have its own shape. Think about helium when it fills up a balloon. The helium takes the shape of the balloon that it fills.

**Directions:** Look at each picture. Circle the correct state of matter.

| 1. | | **a.** solid |
| | | **b.** liquid |
| | | **c.** gas |
| 2. | | **a.** solid |
| | | **b.** liquid |
| | | **c.** gas |
| 3. | | **a.** solid |
| | | **b.** liquid |
| | | **c.** gas |
| 4. | | **a.** solid |
| | | **b.** liquid |
| | | **c.** gas |
| 5. | | **a.** solid |
| | | **b.** liquid |
| | | **c.** gas |

# Show What You Know About Matter

**Directions:** Use the Word Bank below to help answer each question.

| Word Bank | | |
| --- | --- | --- |
| matter | mass | gravity |
| solid | liquid | gas |

1. All matter has _____.

2. Everything is made up of _____.

3. When matter does not change forms, it is called a _____.

4. Water and milk are examples of matter that is a _____.

5. _____ is what gives mass its weight.

6. Air is an example of matter that is a _____.

**Something Extra:** In the space below, draw an example of two different states of matter. Choose from solid, liquid, or gas. Label your drawings.

_____          _____

# Move It

A push or pull makes something move or change its direction. A push or pull is known as a **force**. Earth has a special force called gravity. **Gravity** is what pulls things toward the Earth.

Why is gravity so important? Without gravity, things would simply float away. If you want to see gravity in action, hold out a pencil and let it go. Gravity will pull the pencil to the ground.

Gravity pulls things, but sometimes a person needs help to move something. A person might use a simple machine to help move an object. Think about a person in a wheelchair. A ramp is helpful to move the person up or down a small hill. This ramp is a simple machine that helps with pulling or pushing the wheelchair down or up the hill.

**Directions:** Circle the correct answer and write it on the line. _____

1. A push is a type of _____.

    **a.** gravity                              **b.** force

2. A pull is a type of _____.

    **a.** force                              **b.** gravity

3. Gravity is an important force because it _____.

    **a.** pulls things toward Earth        **b.** pushes things away from Earth

4. A simple machine can help _____.

    **a.** stop an object                    **b.** move an object

5. An example of a simple machine is _____.

    **a.** gravity                              **b.** a ramp

# Push or Pull?

**Directions:** Look at each picture. Label the motion as a **push** or a **pull**.

# What Path Does It Take?

When an object moves, it moves in a **path**. Complete the activity below to learn more about the path an object can take.

**Directions:** Color the picture that shows the correct path.

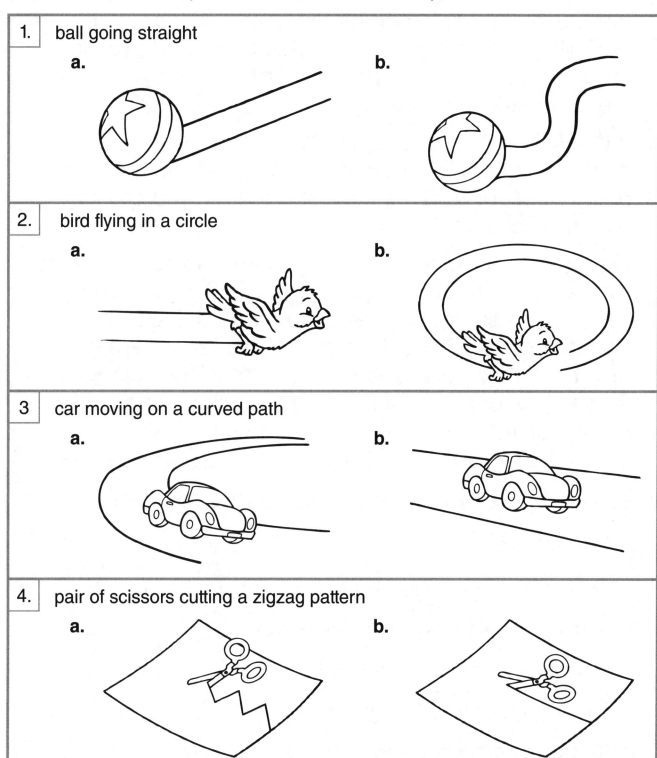

1. ball going straight

   a.

   b.

2. bird flying in a circle

   a.

   b.

3 car moving on a curved path

   a.

   b.

4. pair of scissors cutting a zigzag pattern

   a.

   b.

# The Days and Nights

Earth **rotates** or spins on its axis. This rotation causes day and night on Earth. The sun is the closest star to the Earth. As the Earth rotates toward the sun, the part of Earth facing the sun has daylight. As Earth rotates away from the sun, the part of Earth facing away from the sun has darkness.

It takes 24 hours for Earth to finish one rotation. This is why there are 24 hours in one day. Sometimes it is hard to believe Earth is moving because you cannot feel the movement.

One great way to see how this works is to have a friend hold a flashlight and point the light on a globe. The flashlight is like the sun, and the globe is like Earth. Spin the globe but hold the flashlight steady. Watch how the light changes where it lands as Earth moves. This is how our closest star, the sun, shines on our planet Earth.

**Directions:** Use the paragraphs above to help fill in the blanks below.

1. Earth rotates on its_____ .

2. Earth's rotation causes day and_____ .

3. The part of Earth facing away from the sun has _____.

4. For Earth to finish one rotation, it takes _____.

5. Earth is always moving, but you cannot feel it _____.

6. The closest star to Earth is the _____.

# A Part of the Solar System

## Part 1

**Directions:** Label and color the four planets that are closest to the sun.

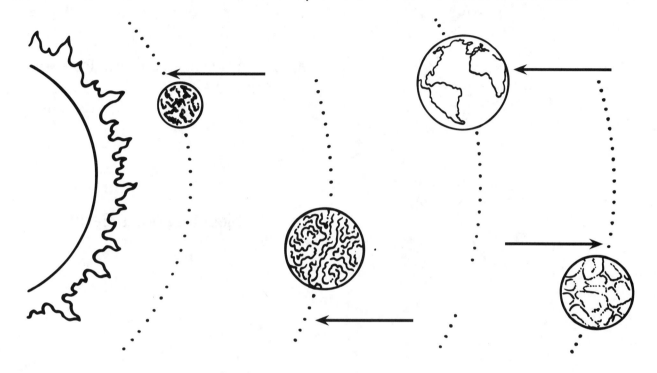

## Part 2

**Directions:** Label and color the four outer planets.

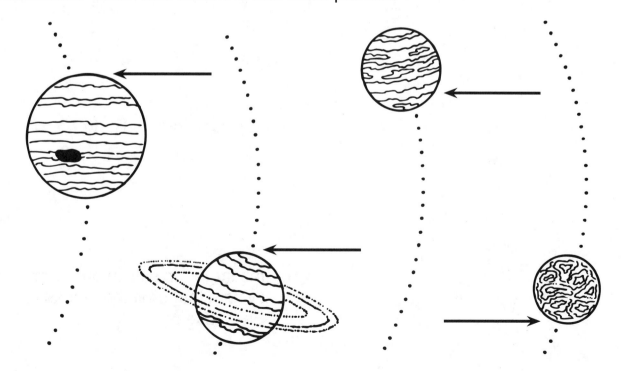

# Earth's Neighbors

**Directions:** Draw a line to match each picture to its definition.

1.

    **a.** bright balls of gas that are seen from the sky

2.

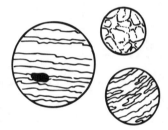

    **b.** the object that orbits Earth

3.

    **c.** patterns in the sky made of stars

4.

    **d.** the closet star to Earth

5.

    **e.** the larger objects in our solar system that orbit the sun as Earth does

# Moon Phases

The moon goes through phases. The **new moon** is the first phase. The **first quarter moon** is the second phase. The third phase is called a **full moon**. Finally, the last phase is called the **third quarter moon**.

**Directions:** Look at the pictures of four of the moon's phases. The phases are not in order. The hatch marks (slanted lines) on the moon show the phase. Hatch marks mean that that part of the moon cannot be seen.

—On the line under each picture, write a number (1, 2, 3, or 4) to put the phases of the moon in order. The new moon should be number 1.

—On the line above each picture, write the name of the phase of the moon.

# Answer Key for Second Grade

**Page 13**
1. I like school because it is fun.
2. Do you see the stars in the sky?
3. I wish I had a new toy.
4. The animals in the woods moved quietly through the trees.
5. Please fix our supper so we can hurry up and eat.

**Page 14**
1. a    2. b    3. b    4. a
5. b    6. b    7. b    8. b

**Page 15**
1. a    2. a    3. b    4. a    5. b
6. b    7. c    8. b    9. a    10. a
11. a    12. c    13. b    14. a    15. a

**Page 16**
1. friend, circus    2. money, wallet
3. horse, cow, barn    4. Jason, kitten, fish
5. cake, pie, cookies    6. doctor, sticker
7. Steve, ticket    8. pizza, pickles
9. library, place    10. dog, fleas
*Something Extra:* Answers will vary.

**Page 17**
*Foods*
1. pizza    2. candy    3. cheese    4. bread
*Places*
1. store    2. school    3. hospital    4. kitchen
*Animals*
1. horse    2. bear    3. lion    4. cat
*People*
1. nurse    2. doctor    3. teacher    4. mother
*Something Extra:* Answers will vary.

**Page 18**

| Singular | Plural |
|----------|--------|
| 1. dog | dogs |
| 2. car | cars |
| 3. house | houses |
| 4. pencil | pencils |
| 5. bean | beans |
| 6. plate | plates |
| 7. juice | juices |
| 8. apple | apples |
| 9. fan | fans |
| 10. phone | phones |

**Page 19**

| Part 1 | | Part 2 | |
|--------|--------|--------|--------|
| 1. shoes | 2. cats | 1. kid | 2. horse |
| 3. trees | 4. trucks | 3. clock | 4. plant |
| 5. boats | 6. barns | 5. basket | 6. girl |

**Page 20**
1. sit    2. speak    3. walk    4. eat
5. go    6. talk    7. sew    8. jump
9. laugh    10. smile

**Page 21**
1. Run    2. Walk    3. Take    4. Tell
5. Moves    6. Go    7. Watch    8. Jump
9. Sit    10. Cry

**Page 22**
*Should be colored:* tell, grow, make, go, talk, run, look, stop, sing, bake

**Page 23**
1. happy    2. fluffy    3. nice
4. sweet    5. beautiful    6. short
7. helpful    8. mean

**Page 24**
1. nice    2. cute    3. ugly
4. pointy    5. sweet    6. bumpy
7. sharp    8. smooth    9. sad
10. tall    11. little    12. quick
13. wet    14. hot

**Page 25**
*Part 1*
1. new    2. best    3. sweet
4. stormy    5. red    6. fluffy
*Part 2:* Answers will vary.

**Page 26**
1. ugly    2. sweet    5. silly
6. salty    7. nice    9. sunny
10. tiny    11. short    12. funny
14. bright    16. dark    17. shiny

**Page 27**
*Part 1*
1. b    2. a    3. a    4. b    5. b
*Part 2:* Answers will vary.

**Page 28**
1. swiftly    2. so
3. there    4. Today
5. so    6. Answers will vary.

**Page 29**
1. n., v., adv.
2. adj., adj., n., v., adv.
3. n., v., adj., n.
4. adj., adj., n., v., adv., adv.
5. n., v., n., adj., adj., n.
6. n., adv., v., adj., adj., n.
7. n., v., adj., adj., n.
8. adj., adj., n., v., adv.
9. n., v., n., adj., adj., n.
10. n., v., adj., adj., n.

# Answer Key for Second Grade (cont.)

**Page 30**

*nouns:* monkey, boy, man, cow
*verbs:* go, run, jump, swim
*adjectives:* pretty, funny, silly, nice
*adverbs:* slowly, quickly, very, too

**Page 31**

*Should be colored:* balloon, town, about, past, little, soft, people, brave, eraser, brick, new, write, brother
*Should be rewritten:* cloud, pencil, pretty, street, dancer, happy, sister, candy

**Page 32**

Definitions will vary slightly.

1. airplane
2. juggler
3. apple
4. orange
5. onion
6. puppy

**Page 33**

*Part 1*

| blue | | red | |
|------|------|------|------|
| 1. brake | 5. time | 1. chop | 5. kid |
| 2. bake | 6. bite | 2. set | 6. sip |
| 3. side | 7. kite | 3. chip | 7. big |
| 4. tide | 8. cake | 4. tip | 8. dip |

*Part 2:* Answers will vary.

**Page 34**

1. near
2. wonderful
3. whole
4. large
5. faster
6. kind

**Page 35**

1. little, big
2. nice, mean
3. fast, slow
4. sweet, sour
5. dull, shiny
6. hard, easy
7. up, down
8. never, always
9. nervous, calm
10. glad, sad

**Page 36**

1. a
2. a
3. b
4. a
5. a
6. b
7. b
8. a

**Page 37**

1. a
2. b
3. c
4. a
5. b
6. c
7. b
8. a

**Page 38**

*Correctly capitalized:* Jason Hunter, Kate Owen, Tim Boyd, Pam Winters, Sandy Evans
*Corrected names:* Doctor Morgan, Paula Brown, Mrs. Parks, Mr. Carter

**Page 39**

1. I don't know what time it is.
2. She is a very nice person.
3. Can we go to the playground?
4. Today is a beautiful day.
5. How old are you?

**Page 40**

1. a. She          b. Dr.
2. a. When          b. Lisa's

3. a. I          b. Sandy
4. a. My          b. Spencer
5. a. Can          b. Carla

**Page 41**

*Part 1*

1. .     2. .     3. .     4. .     5. .

*Part 2:* Answers will vary; however, all sentences must end with a period.

**Page 42**

*Part 1*

1. ?     2. ?     3. ?     4. ?     5. ?

*Part 2:* Answers will vary; however, all sentences must end with a question mark.

**Page 43**

1. ?     2. .     3. .     4. ?     5. .
6. .     7. ?     8. .     9. .     10. ?

**Page 44**

1. I went to the math class, reading class, and spelling class.
2. Please bring me my coat, my umbrella, and my purse.
3. My favorite days are Friday, Saturday, and Sunday.
4. June, July, and August are summer months.
5. Mercury, Venus, and Earth are planets that are close to the sun.
6. Red, orange, and yellow are all colors in the rainbow.
7. Please get some milk, donuts, and cereal at the store.
8. For camping you will need a sleeping bag, a flashlight, and some food.
9. Three people I admire are my mother, my father, and my grandmother.
10. After school we need to stop at the post office, the grocery store, and the bank.

**Page 45**

1. he's
2. she's
3. hasn't
4. won't
5. he'd
6. should've
7. would've
8. they're
9. I'm
10. they'll

**Page 46**

1. a
2. b
3. b
4. a
5. a
6. b
7. a
8. b

**Page 47**

Beginnings will vary.

1. dogs, fish, and turtles
2. pizza, hamburgers, and hot dogs
3. red, white, and blue
4. October, November, and December
5. Florida, California, and Texas

# Answer Key for Second Grade *(cont.)*

**Page 47** *(cont.)*

6. small, tiny, and little
7. pants, shirts, and shoes
8. gum, candy, and mints
9. helicopters, airplanes, and hot air balloons
10. eyes, nose, and mouth

**Page 48**

1. She is nice, sweet, and pretty.
2. C
3. I have lived in Texas, Utah, and Virginia.
4. My favorite subjects are art, math, and music.
5. C
6. My favorite numbers are three, eight, and nine.
7. The teacher asked us to bring our books, our pencils, and our papers.
8. C
9. January, February, and March are very cold months.
10. I wish I could have a cat, a dog, and a hamster.

**Page 49**

Once upon a time there was a sweet, beautiful, young princess named Leiana.

She loved the butterflies, the flowers, and the sunshine.

She saw some birds, one snake, and a brown rabbit.

She wished she could stay outside all the time like the lucky birds, snakes, and rabbits.

I could give you jewels, silver, or gold.

If she changed places with the frog, she could be outside in the winter, spring, summer, and fall.

The cook thought it odd that the princess wanted flies, bugs, and worms for supper, but of course, he didn't say anything.

Well, that night she croaked, and croaked, and croaked with joy because she finally had everything she had always wanted!

**Page 50**

1. April 26, 1930
2. June 8, 1991
3. September 12, 2000
4. March 3, 1997
5. December 28, 1966
6. July 4, 1776
7. January 1, 2009
8. February 19, 1967
9. October 27, 2005
10. August 3, 1918
11. May 15, 1945
12. November 10, 1772

**Page 51**

1. I was born on February 25, 2001.
2. School started on August 4, 2008.
3. The picture was taken March 7, 1981.
4. The war began on April 7, 1939.
5. The date on the coin was January 5, 1977.
6. December 25, 1977, is the date of my parents' anniversary.
7. He plans to graduate from high school on May 3, 2011.
8. Her grandmother was born on February 25, 1911.
9. July 4, 1776, is an important date in America's history.
10. The movie was shown for the first time on March 4, 1999.
11. Jane flew on a plane for the first time on June 18, 2007.
12. The last time the circus came to town was July 15, 2009.

**Page 52**

1. Austin, Texas
2. Hollywood, California
3. Seattle, Washington
4. Memphis, Tennessee
5. Louisville, Kentucky
6. Ogden, Utah
7. Las Vegas, Nevada
8. Atlanta, Georgia
9. Destin, Florida
10. St. Louis, Missouri

*Something Extra:* Answers will vary.

**Page 53**

Answers will vary slightly.

**Page 54**

Answers will vary.

**Page 55**

1. Puppy Power
2. page 97
3. 27
4. How to buy the perfect gift for your pet
5. Answers will vary.

**Page 56**

1. girl
2. dog
3. swings or swing set
4. sand or dirt

**Page 57**

Answers will vary slightly.

**Page 58**

Answers will vary.

# Answer Key for Second Grade *(cont.)*

**Page 59**
Answers will vary slightly.

**Page 60**
Answers will vary slightly.

**Page 61**
1. a          2. b          3. a          4. b

**Page 62**
*Part 1*
1. 4, 5, 6
2. April, May, June
3. D, E, F
4. summer, fall
5. Thursday, Friday, Saturday

*Part 2:* Answers will vary.

**Page 63**
1. c, b, d, a          2. b, a, d, c

**Page 64**
1. acorn, acre, animal, ant, apple
2. sand, seven, spin, stop, summer
3. table, tiger, time, tree, triangle
4. call, camp, car, clam, collar

**Page 65**
1. b, c, a          2. a, c, b
3. a, c, b          4. a, b, c

**Page 66**
*Part 1:* Answers will vary.
*Part 2:* Answers will vary.
*Part 3:* Answers will vary.

**Page 67**
1. My new puppy jumped onto my lap.
2. The little boy ate the ice cream.
3. The monkey swung from a vine.
4. My sister plays soccer and softball.

*Something Extra:* Answers will vary.

**Page 68**
1. kite          2. cake          3. tree          4. box
5. walk          6. airplane          7. road

**Page 69**
Answers will vary.

**Page 70**
Answers will slightly vary.
1. Kim and Kelly are looking forward to the weekend and their day at the playground.
2. The rain makes Kim and Kelly sad.
3. Their mother plans a special day inside for the girls.

*Something Extra:* Answers will vary.

**Page 71**
*Corrected words:* Friday, Saturday, December, PM, PM, Pedro, Elizabeth

*Something Extra:* Answers will vary.

**Page 72**
Correct order: 3, 4, 1, 2

**Page 73**
*Part 1:* Answers will vary.
*Part 2:* Answers will vary.

**Page 74**
List 1: bread          List 2: January
List 3: glue           List 4: pumpkin
List 5: toy            List 6: car

**Page 75**
1. b          2. c          3. a
*Something Extra:* Answers will vary.

**Page 76**
1. 12     2. 15     3. 20     4. 4     5. 17
6. 5      7. 6      8. 10     9. 9     10. 8

**Page 77**
Answers will vary.

**Page 78**
1. 3, 6, 7              2. 13, 14, 15
3. 8, 10, 12           4. 22, 24, 26
5. 16, 17, 18, 21      6. 34, 36, 38
7. 19, 21, 23, 24      8. 47, 49, 50, 51
9. 39, 41, 43, 45      10. 50, 53, 54, 56

**Page 79**
1. 20, 30, 35          2. 45, 60, 65
3. 10, 20, 30          4. 40, 45, 55
5. 70, 80, 85, 90      6. 25, 35, 50
7. 10, 20, 30          8. 80, 90, 100
9. 50, 60, 65          10. 20, 25, 35

**Page 80**
*Part 1*
Groups 1, 3, 4, and 6 should be colored.
*Part 2*
1. 5 jelly beans          2. 10 squares
3. 15 hearts

**Page 81**
1. 30, 50     2. 40, 60     3. 55, 85
4. 40, 50     5. 45, 65     6. 60, 80
7. 35, 45     8. 80, 90     9. 42, 62
10. 50, 70

**Page 82**
1. 20     2. 70     3. 30     4. 50     5. 70

**Page 83**
*Part 1*                   *Part 2*
1. 70, 60                  1. 65, 45
2. 10                      2. 70, 60
3. 20                      3. 55, 35
4. 40, 30                  4. 57, 37
5. 50, 40                  5. 85, 65

# Answer Key for Second Grade *(cont.)*

**Page 84**

| | | |
|---|---|---|
| a. O | b. E | c. E |
| d. O | e. E | f. O |
| g. O | h. E | i. O |
| j. O | k. E | l. O |

**Page 85**

Answers for the estimates may vary. Discuss estimates with students.

| | | |
|---|---|---|
| 1. 30 | 2. 50 | 3. 10 |
| 4. 30 | 5. 50 | 6. 10 |

**Page 86**

| | | | |
|---|---|---|---|
| 1. 5 | 2. 30 | 3. 15 | 4. 20 |
| 5. 40 | 6. 30 | 7. 20 | 8. 5 |

**Page 87**

1. >    2. <    3. <    4. >    5. >

**Page 88**

| | | | | |
|---|---|---|---|---|
| 1. < | 2. < | 3. > | 4. < | 5. > |
| 6. < | 7. < | 8. > | 9. < | 10. < |

**Page 89**

| | | |
|---|---|---|
| 1. a. 7 | b. 15 | c. 10, 11, 12 |
| 2. a. 5 | b. 1 | c. 2, 3, 4 |
| 3. a. 21 | b. 20 | c. 22 |

**Page 90**

| | | |
|---|---|---|
| 1. a. 10, 20 | b. 30, 40, 50 | c. 20 |
| 2. a. 4 | b. 4, 5 | c. 2 |
| 3. a. 15, 20, 25 | b. 5 | c. 10, 15, 20 |
| 4. a. 21 | b. 22, 23, 24 | c. 20, 21 |

**Page 91**

*Part 1*
1. 1st/first
2. 2nd/second
3. 3rd/third

*Part 2*
1. 6
2. 10
3. 6

**Page 92**

**Page 93**

1. 12   2. 10   3. 11   4. 13   5. 14   6. 12

*Something Extra:* Answers will vary.

**Page 94**

| | | | | |
|---|---|---|---|---|
| 1. 7 | 2. 16 | 3. 13 | 4. 14 | 5. 9 |
| 6. 13 | 7. 14 | 8. 9 | 9. 19 | 10. 13 |

**Page 95**

| | | | |
|---|---|---|---|
| 1. 8, 8 | 2. 14, 14 | 3. 9, 9 | 4. 17, 17 |
| 5. 5, 5 | 6. 14, 14 | 7. 7, 7 | 8. 11, 11 |

**Page 96**

| | | | |
|---|---|---|---|
| 1. 45 | 2. 47 | 3. 75 | 4. 80 |
| 5. 38 | 6. 99 | 7. 69 | 8. 89 |
| 9. 29 | 10. 98 | 11. 67 | 12. 89 |

**Page 97**

*Part 1*

| | | | |
|---|---|---|---|
| 1. 489 | 2. 799 | 3. 290 | 4. 918 |
| 5. 994 | 6. 666 | 7. 318 | 8. 839 |
| 9. 299 | 10. 988 | 11. 995 | 12. 881 |

*Part 2* 449 students

**Page 98**

| | | | |
|---|---|---|---|
| 1. 7 | 2. 1 | 3. 2 | 4. 4 |
| 5. 2 | 6. 2 | 7. 1 | 8. 1 |
| 9. 3 | 10. 5 | 11. 1 | 12. 3 |

**Page 99**

*Part 1*

| | | | |
|---|---|---|---|
| 1. 20 | 2. 51 | 3. 33 | 4. 34 |
| 5. 11 | 6. 27 | 7. 62 | 8. 10 |
| 9. 6 | 10. 47 | 11. 21 | 12. 40 |

*Part 2* 22 people

**Page 100**

*Part 1*

| | | |
|---|---|---|
| 1. 441 | 2. 128 | 3. 200 |
| 4. 141 | 5. 221 | 6. 101 |
| 7. 411 | 8. 380 | 9. 211 |
| 10. 521 | 11. 300 | 12. 252 |

*Part 2* 182 cans

**Page 101**

| | | | | |
|---|---|---|---|---|
| 1. 17 | 2. 29 | 3. 28 | 4. 16 | 5. 29 |
| 6. 19 | 7. 3 | 8. 18 | 9. 16 | 10. 9 |

**Page 102**

| | | |
|---|---|---|
| 1. 5, 2 | 2. 10, 6 | 3. 8, 7 |
| 4. 8, 4 | 5. 14, 6 | 6. 17, 9 |
| 7. 15, 12 | 8. 12, 7 | |

**Page 103**

| | | | |
|---|---|---|---|
| 1. 3 | 2. 9 | 3. 9 | 4. 3 |
| 5. 2 | 6. 6 | 7. 10 | 8. 10 |
| 9. 7 | 10. 7 | 11. 5 | 12. 13 |

*Addition problems:* 2, 3, 7, 8, 9, 10, 12
*Subtraction problems:* 1, 4, 5, 6, 11

**Page 104**

| | | |
|---|---|---|
| 1. 64 | 2. 9 | 3. 41 |
| 4. 78 | 5. 21 | 6. 58 |
| 7. 21 | 8. 50 | 9. 49 |
| 10. 45 | 11. 60 | 12. 51 |
| 13. 62 | 14. 48 | 15. 89 |

# Answer Key for Second Grade *(cont.)*

**Page 105**

1. b    2. a    3. b    4. a    5. b

**Page 106**

1. 7
2. Sunday
3. Wednesday
4. December 4 and December 6
5. Tuesday
6. 4
7. Sunday

**Page 107**

1. a   2. a   3. a   4. b   5. a   6. b

**Page 108**

1. 3:00    2. 7:00    3. 4:00    4. 12:00
5. 10:00   6. 1:00    7. 5:00    8. 2:00

**Page 109**

1. 11:00  2. 1:00    3. 4:00    4. 10:00
5. 12:00  6. 2:00    7. 5:00    8. 9:00

**Page 110**

| 1. 10:00 | 2. 2:00 |
| 3. 5:00 | 4. 7:00 |
| 5. 11:00 | 6. 3:00 |
| 7. 4:00 | 8. 1:00 |

**Page 111**

| 1. 6:30 | 2. half past two |
| 3. three-thirty | 4. 30 minutes after one |
| 5. half past twelve | 6. 5:30 |
| 7. 11:30 | 8. half past ten |

**Page 112**

1. 7:35    2. 12:15    3. 8:05
4. 6:20    5. 5:50    6. 10:25

**Page 113**

1. 25 cents   4. 60 cents   7. 50 cents
2. 36 cents   5. 35 cents   8. 70 cents
3. 50 cents   6. 85 cents

**Page 114**

1. a   2. b   3. a   4. b

**Page 115**

1. >  2. <  3. >  4. >  5. >  6. <

**Page 116**

1. $5.00    2. $4.00    3. $7.50

**Page 117**

1. coin, bubble, needle   3. carrot, pencil
2. feather              4. crayon

*Something Extra:* Answers will vary.

**Page 118**

1. feather—8 cm   4. stick of gum—3 cm
2. bug—2 cm     5. circle—1 cm
3. worm—6 cm    6. ribbon —4 cm

**Page 119**

*more* than a pound: car, horse, house, computer

*less* than a pound: feather, bug, ribbon, dollar bill, piece of paper

*Something Extra:* Answers will vary.

**Page 120**

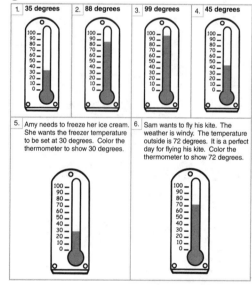

**Page 121**

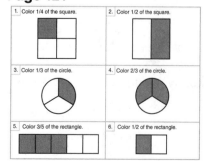

*Something Extra:* 3/4 of the square is colored.

# Answer Key for Second Grade *(cont.)*

**Page 122**
1. 3/7 cats, 4/7 dogs
2. 3/7 bowls, 4/7 cones
3. 5/10 no flowers, 5/10 with flowers

*Something Extra:* 2/6 squares, 4/6 triangles

**Page 123**

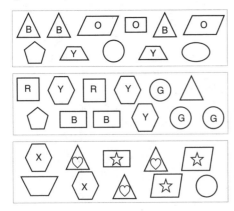

**Page 124**

*Part 1*
1. 2nd and 3rd items should be blue.
2. 1st and 4th items should be orange.
3. 1st and 2nd items should be red.

*Part 2*
1. cube    2. rectangular prism    3. sphere

**Page 125**
1. a    2. a    3. a    4. b
5. b    6. a    7. a    8. b

**Page 126**

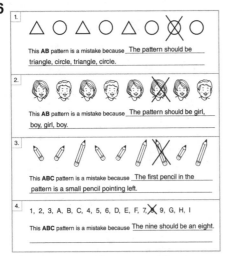

Students' explanations will vary. Check for accuracy.

**Page 127**
Check that students have completed the patterns correctly.

**Page 128**
1. Favorite Colors    2. 20
3. red    4. 5
5. blue    6. 4

**Page 129**
1. Kate's School Reading Journal
2. the number of pages read each night
3. Thursday
4. Monday and Wednesday
5. 80 pages

**Page 130**
1. Piney Woods Campground
2. The key explains how to read the symbols on the map.
3. 2
4. 4
5. It is for the playground.

**Page 131**

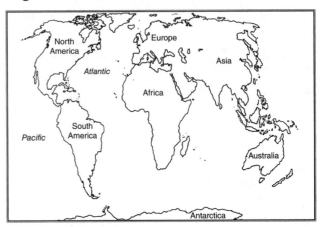

Check students' coloring and responses.

**Page 132**
1. North America    2. south
3. Antarctica    4. north
5. Europe    6. South America

**Page 133**

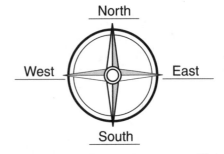

*Something Extra:* Answers will vary.

**Page 134**
1. north    2. south    3. south and east
4. north and west    5. north and west

**Page 135**
1–3. Check coloring.
4. Pacific and Atlantic
5. The United States of America

# Answer Key for Second Grade *(cont.)*

**Page 136**
1. a    2. a    3. a    4. b    5. b    6. a

**Page 137**
*Part 1*
1. globe
2. compass rose
3. map key
4. equator
5. continents
6. oceans

*Part 2*
Europe, Asia, Africa, Australia, North America, South America, Antarctica (in any order)

**Page 138**
1. a       2. b       3. a
4. a       5. a       6. b

**Page 139**
1. 1789
2. the War of 1812
3. the Civil War ends
4. Britain
5. 1776
6. the signing of the Declaration of Independence

**Page 140**
1. b    2. d    3. a    4. e    5. c

**Page 141**
1. the Indians
2. He thought he was in India.
3. They might have walked across a land bridge from Asia to the Americas.
4. yes
5. to search or hunt for food
6. Earth

**Page 142**
1. free
2. England
3. England
4. religious freedom, to own land, to make money (any two)
5. voice/say
6. Revolutionary War

**Page 143**
1. b    2. b    3. b    4. a    5. a    6. a

**Page 144**
1. government
2. laws
3. local, state, national
4. citizens
5. leaders
6. rights and freedoms
*Something Extra:* Answers will vary.

**Page 145**
1. to help Eastside Elementary get new playground equipment and/or to help people clean up by recycling
2. answers will vary slightly—because they are recycling and helping children
3. Eastside Elementary
4. playground equipment
5. aluminum cans and newspapers

**Page 146**
1. 23
2. 13
3. 10
4. the zoo
5. Answers will vary.

**Page 147**
1. 13
2. the original 13 colonies
3. the states
4. 50
5. red, white, blue

**Page 148**

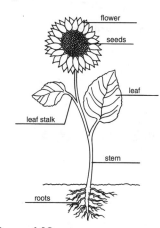

**Page 149**
*Should be colored:* water, sunlight, soil, plant food

**Page 150**
1. a                    2. a
3. a                    4. b
*Something Extra:* Answers will vary.

**Page 151**
*mammals:* dog, cow
*reptiles:* turtle, alligator, snake
*amphibians:* salamander, frog
*birds:* ostrich, penguin, eagle

**Page 152**
1. b          2. a          3. a          4. b
*Something Extra:* Answers will vary.

# Answer Key for Second Grade *(cont.)*

## Page 153
Answers will vary. Check illustrations.

## Page 154
1. sun
2. 365 days
3. one year
4. seasons
5. toward
6. away
7. equator
8. warm/hot

## Page 155

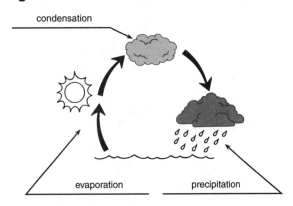

*Something Extra:* Answers will vary.

## Page 156
Answers will vary.

## Page 157
1. The United States
2. sunny
3. Yes, because they are going to have snow.
4. the West
5. Answers will vary.

## Page 158
1. b      2. a      3. b      4. a

## Page 159
1. b    2. a    3. c    4. a    5. c

## Page 160
1. mass
2. matter
3. solid
4. liquid
5. Gravity
6. gas

*Something Extra:* Answers will vary.

## Page 161
1. b    2. a    3. a    4. b    5. b

## Page 162
1. push          2. pull
3. push          4. push
5. pull          6. pull

## Page 163
1. a          2. b
3. a          4. a

## Page 164
1. axis
2. night
3. night
4. 24 hours
5. move
6. sun

## Page 165

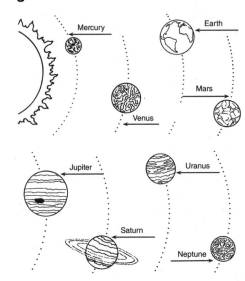

## Page 166
1. d      2. e      3. b      4. c      5. a

## Page 167

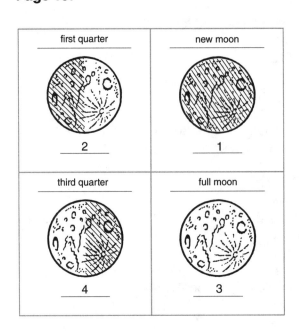

# Bonus Section

This section offers a jump start
for third-grade skills in
language arts and math for
those second-grade students
who are ready to move ahead.

# Common and Proper Nouns

You already know a noun is a person, place, or thing. Now it is time to learn there are different types of nouns. Some nouns are common nouns, and some nouns are proper nouns.

**Examples**

A **common noun** is not specific.
Common nouns are not capitalized.
   boy → common noun

A **proper noun** is specific.
Proper nouns are always capitalized.
   Brett → proper noun

**Directions:** Look at each common noun. Write a proper noun that is more specific than the common noun given.

1. month     _____

2. girl     _____

3. holiday     _____

4. restaurant     _____

5. teacher     _____

6. student     _____

7. store     _____

8. country     _____

9. city     _____

10. state     _____

# Connecting Words

**Conjunctions** are words that connect other words in a sentence. The most common conjunctions are *and, but, or, nor, for,* and *yet.*

**Directions:** Circle the best conjunction for each sentence. Write the correct conjunction on the line.

1. I want to go, _____ I already have other plans.

   **a.** but

   **b.** nor

2. Either Tim _____ Jim should be given the award.

   **a.** for

   **b.** or

3. She is my cousin, _____ she is also my friend.

   **a.** and

   **b.** for

4. Neither Kristen _____ Allison knew what time the play started.

   **a.** and

   **b.** nor

5. He is nice, _____ sometimes he can be mean.

   **a.** yet

   **b.** nor

# What You Say

When a person's exact words are written down, they are placed inside quotation marks.

> **Examples**
>
> Ann said, "How are you today?"
>
> Crede replied, "I am just fine."

Only the words Ann and Crede actually said are placed inside the quotation marks.

**Directions:** Look at the following sentences. Add quotation marks where needed. **Hint:** There is one mistake in each sentence.

1. Jett said, "Kevin is my best friend.

2. Do you have any gum?" Sandy asked.

3. "How old are you? Kate asked.

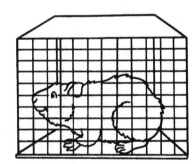

4. I wish I had a pet hamster," Linda said.

5. Someone needs to clean up this mess," the teacher said.

6. "I'm so proud of you! her mother exclaimed.

7. "I don't like to watch a lot of television, Ken said.

8. "Tessa, please hang up the phone, Simon said.

9. "Where are you going on vacation? asked Mrs. Smith.

10. I have enough time to get this finished," she said.

# Figurative Language

Sometimes when people speak they do not mean exactly what they are saying. This kind of speech is called **figurative language**.

> **Examples**
>
> She is stubborn as a mule.
>
> She is an angel!

No one is really a mule or an angel. This is simply figurative language. It is just another way to express one's thoughts.

**Directions:** Circle the part of the sentence that shows figurative language. Explain what you think it means.

1. My brother is as messy as a pig.

   _____

2. The baby is as cute as a button!

   _____

3. He is as fast as the wind.

   _____

4. I'm so hungry I could eat a cow!

   _____

5. She sounds like she has a frog in her throat.

   _____

6. He is a little devil!

   _____

**Something Extra:** Choose one of the sentences above and use the space on the back of this page to draw a picture of what is being said. For example, if the figurative expression said "she had butterflies in her stomach," then draw a picture of a girl with butterflies in her belly.

# Tongue Twisters

**Alliteration** is repeating the same consonant sound at the beginning of words. The best examples of alliteration are familiar tongue twisters such as "Peter Piper picked a peck of pickled peppers" or "She sells sea shells down by the seashore."

## Part 1

**Directions:** Finish each alliteration. **Hint:** An alliteration can use some other sounds, but it should stick to mainly one sound.

1. Mad Mandy made Mildred meet _____

   _____ .

2. Please prepare more pumpkin_____

   _____ .

3. Kelly can carefully cook _____

   _____ .

## Part 2

**Directions:** Underline the words that share the same sounds.

1. My mother makes me many meals.

2. Does David drive Dawn downtown?

3. Can Kara cook caramel apples?

**Something Extra:** On the back of this page, write an alliteration of your own.

_____

_____

# Cursive Sentences

**Directions:** Practice writing in cursive by rewriting the following sentences.

1. My mother is the greatest mother in the world.

   _____

   _____

2. Today's weather is better than yesterday's weather.

   _____

   _____

3. Did you see the quick, brown fox jump over the fence?

   _____

   _____

4. I think second grade is the best!

   _____

   _____

5. My birthday is next Friday.

   _____

   _____

# Another Way to End

There are three types of ending punctuation. These are the period, the question mark, and the exclamation mark.

**Examples**

A **period** is for a statement or mild command.

Today is Sunday.          Please, go to the store.

A **question mark** is for asking a question.

How are you doing?          Did you sleep well?

An **exclamation mark** shows excitement.

How lovely the moon is!     I am eight years old today!

**Directions:** Read each sentence. Add the correct ending punctuation.

1. My father is a teacher ___

2. How lovely your dress is ___

3. Do you know what time it is ___

4. Why aren't you going with us ___

5. The house is on fire _____

6. Please give me my book ____

7. Why are you here _____

8. I like chocolate ____

9. Go to the office right away ___

10. I am going to the store ____

# Adding with Decimals

When you add numbers with decimals, you do not move the decimal.

| **Examples** | 72.19 | $1.05 |
|---|---|---|
| | + 12.10 | + 0.62 |
| | 84.29 | $1.67 |

## Part 1

**Directions:** Add each problem to find the sum.

1.
$$\begin{array}{r} 12.89 \\ + \ 10.10 \\ \hline \end{array}$$

2.
$$\begin{array}{r} 5.13 \\ + \ 71.02 \\ \hline \end{array}$$

3.
$$\begin{array}{r} 0.41 \\ + \ 11.13 \\ \hline \end{array}$$

4.
$$\begin{array}{r} 6.31 \\ + \ 21.18 \\ \hline \end{array}$$

5.
$$\begin{array}{r} 33.19 \\ + \ 21.10 \\ \hline \end{array}$$

6.
$$\begin{array}{r} 39.34 \\ + \ 10.02 \\ \hline \end{array}$$

7.
$$\begin{array}{r} 71.23 \\ + \ 21.12 \\ \hline \end{array}$$

8.
$$\begin{array}{r} 20.20 \\ + \ 30.30 \\ \hline \end{array}$$

9.
$$\begin{array}{r} 37.34 \\ + \ 31.35 \\ \hline \end{array}$$

10.
$$\begin{array}{r} 76.21 \\ + \ 23.03 \\ \hline \end{array}$$

## Part 2

**Directions:** Complete each word problem to find the sum.

1. Sam had $23.56 in his bank. His grandfather gave him $11.00 for his birthday. How much money does Sam have now?

   Show your work:


   **Answer:** _____

2. Cal bought a shirt that cost $12.62. He also bought a hat that cost $10.12. How much money did Cal spend?

   Show your work:


   **Answer:** _____

# Subtracting with Decimals

When you subtract numbers with decimals, you do not move the decimal.

| **Examples** | 77. 2 | $ 5.56 |
|---|---|---|
| | − 24. 1 | − 1.42 |
| | 53. 1 | $ 4.14 |

**Directions:** Solve each subtraction problem to find the difference.

1.
```
    17.2
 − 14.1
```

2.
```
    38.9
 − 22.2
```

3.
```
    59.8
 − 44.2
```

4.
```
    97.3
 − 37.1
```

5.
```
    76.3
 − 41.3
```

6.
```
    64.9
 − 52.6
```

7.
```
    92.1
 − 31.1
```

8.
```
    76.6
 − 61.5
```

9.
```
    87.7
 − 73.5
```

10.
```
    31.9
 − 20.7
```

# Beginning Multiplication

You already know how to add.  Now it is time to learn to multiply.  Look at the addition problem and compare it to the multiplication problem.

**Examples**

2 + 2 + 2 = 6

2 x 3 = 6

Writing the addition problem as a multiplication problem is shorter and quicker!

**Directions:** Add each addition problem.  Then turn the addition problem into a multiplication problem by writing the correct number in each box.

1.  7 + 7 + 7 + 7 = _____            7 x ☐ = 28

2.  2 + 2 + 2 + 2 + 2 = _____       2 x ☐ = 10

3.  6 + 6 + 6 = _____                6 x ☐ = 18

4.  9 + 9 = _____                    9 x ☐ = 18

5.  3 + 3 + 3 + 3 + 3 + 3 + 3 = _____   3 x ☐ = 21

6.  4 + 4 + 4 + 4 + 4 = _____        4 x ☐ = 20

7.  5 + 5 + 5 = _____                5 x ☐ = 15

8.  8 + 8 = _____                    8 x ☐ = 16

# Divine Division

**Directions:** Find the answer for each division problem.

| | |
|---|---|
| 1. $9 \overline{)\, 81}$ | 2. $10 \overline{)\, 100}$ |
| 3. $7 \overline{)\, 56}$ | 4. $2 \overline{)\, 24}$ |
| 5. $5 \overline{)\, 60}$ | 6. $12 \overline{)\, 36}$ |
| 7. $4 \overline{)\, 12}$ | 8. $8 \overline{)\, 72}$ |
| 9. $5 \overline{)\, 15}$ | 10. $4 \overline{)\, 48}$ |

# See the Connection

Division and multiplication are connected.

**Examples**

$4 \times 3 = 12$

$12 \div 3 = 4$

**Directions:** Work the mixed division and multiplication problems to find the connections.

1.  $7 \times 8 =$ _____     $56 \div 7 =$ _____

2.  $5 \times 6 =$ _____     $30 \div 5 =$ _____

3.  $12 \times 5 =$ _____     $60 \div 12 =$ _____

4.  $4 \times 11 =$ _____     $44 \div 4 =$ _____

5.  $8 \times 2 =$ _____     $16 \div 8 =$ _____

6.  $6 \times 6 =$ _____     $36 \div 6 =$ _____

7.  $9 \times 2 =$ _____     $18 \div 9 =$ _____

8.  $12 \times 4 =$ _____     $48 \div 12 =$ _____

9.  $10 \times 7 =$ _____     $70 \div 10 =$ _____

10.  $3 \times 9 =$ _____     $27 \div 3 =$ _____

# Rounding Numbers

**Directions:** Look at the number that is given. Then look at each set of stars with the numbers written inside of them. Color the star that shows the original number rounded to the nearest 100.

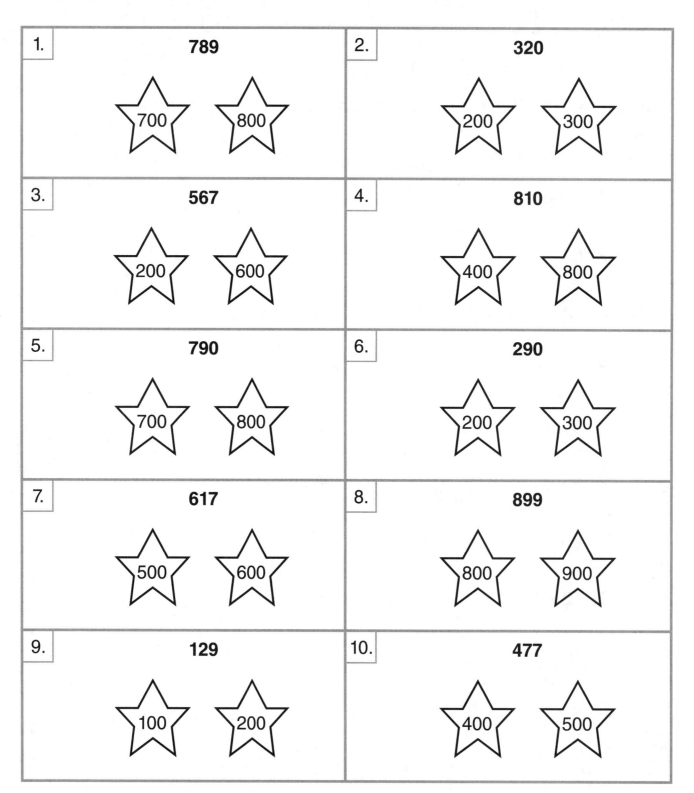

# Learning About Perimeter

The **perimeter** of an object is the total distance around the object. To find the perimeter, measure the sides of the object and then add the numbers together.

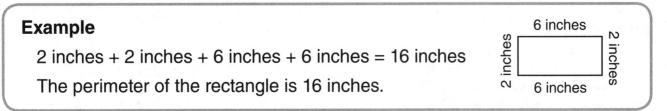

**Example**

2 inches + 2 inches + 6 inches + 6 inches = 16 inches

The perimeter of the rectangle is 16 inches.

**Directions:** Find the perimeter of each object. Circle the correct answer.

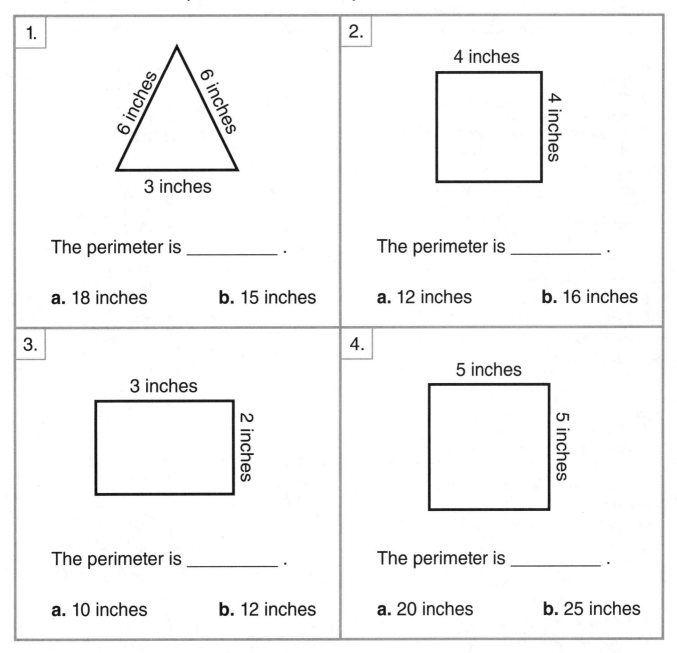

**1.**

6 inches    6 inches

3 inches

The perimeter is _____ .

**a.** 18 inches          **b.** 15 inches

**2.**

4 inches

4 inches

The perimeter is _____ .

**a.** 12 inches          **b.** 16 inches

**3.**

3 inches

2 inches

The perimeter is _____ .

**a.** 10 inches          **b.** 12 inches

**4.**

5 inches

5 inches

The perimeter is _____ .

**a.** 20 inches          **b.** 25 inches

# Answer Key for Bonus Section

**Page 178**
Answers will vary; however, all answers must be capitalized.

**Page 179**
1. a    2. b    3. a    4. b    5. a

**Page 180**
1. Jett said, "Kevin is my best friend."
2. "Do you have any gum?" Sandy asked.
3. "How old are you?" Kate asked.
4. "I wish I had a pet hamster," Linda said.
5. "Someone needs to clean up this mess," the teacher said.
6. "I'm so proud of you!" her mother exclaimed.
7. "I don't like to watch a lot of television," Ken said.
8. "Tessa, please hang up the phone," Simon said.
9. "Where are you going on vacation?" asked Mrs. Smith.
10. "I have enough time to get this finished," she said.

**Page 181**
Answers may vary slightly but must include the following:
1. messy as a pig
2. cute as a button
3. fast as the wind
4. I could eat a cow
5. a frog in her throat
6. little devil

*Something Extra:* Answers will vary.

**Page 182**
*Part 1*
Answers will vary.
*Part 2*
1. All words should be underlined.
2. All words should be underlined.
3. Underline can, Kara, cook, and caramel.

*Something Extra:* Answers will vary.

**Page 183**
Check students' writing.

**Page 184**
1. My father is a teacher.
2. How lovely your dress is!
3. Do you know what time it is?
4. Why aren't you going with us?
5. The house is on fire!

6. Please give me my book.
7. Why are you here?
8. I like chocolate.
9. Go to the office right away!
10. I am going to the store.

**Page 185**
*Part 1*

| | |
|---|---|
| 1. 22.99 | 2. 76.15 |
| 3. 11.54 | 4. 27.49 |
| 5. 54.29 | 6. 49.36 |
| 7. 92.35 | 8. 50.50 |
| 9. 68.69 | 10. 99.24 |

*Part 2*

| | |
|---|---|
| 1. $34.56 | 2. $22.74 |

**Page 186**

| | |
|---|---|
| 1. 3.1 | 2. 16.7 |
| 3. 15.6 | 4. 60.2 |
| 5. 35.0 | 6. 12.3 |
| 7. 61.0 | 8. 15.1 |
| 9. 14.2 | 10. 11.2 |

**Page 187**

| | |
|---|---|
| 1. 28; 4 | 2. 10; 5 |
| 3. 18; 3 | 4. 18; 2 |
| 5. 21; 7 | 6. 20; 5 |
| 7. 15; 3 | 8. 16; 2 |

**Page 188**

| | |
|---|---|
| 1. 9 | 2. 10 |
| 3. 8 | 4. 12 |
| 5. 12 | 6. 3 |
| 7. 3 | 8. 9 |
| 9. 3 | 10. 12 |

**Page 189**

| | |
|---|---|
| 1. 56; 8 | 2. 30; 6 |
| 3. 60; 5 | 4. 44; 11 |
| 5. 16; 2 | 6. 36; 6 |
| 7. 18; 2 | 8. 48; 4 |
| 9. 70; 7 | 10. 27; 9 |

**Page 190**

| | |
|---|---|
| 1. 800 | 2. 300 |
| 3. 600 | 4. 800 |
| 5. 800 | 6. 300 |
| 7. 600 | 8. 900 |
| 9. 100 | 10. 500 |

**Page 191**
1. b
2. b
3. a
4. a